THE COMPLETE GUIDE TO
FLAGS
OF THE WORLD

BRIAN JOHNSON BARKER

CONSULTANT EDITOR: CLIVE CARPENTER

NEW
HOLLAND

NEW
HOLLAND

This edition published in 2009 by New Holland Publishers (UK) Ltd
London • Cape Town • Sydney • Auckland
www.newhollandpublishers.com

Garfield House, 86-88 Edgware Road, London W2 2EA, UK
80 McKenzie Street, Capetown 8001, South Africa
Unit 1, 66 Gibbes Street, Chatswood, NSW 2067, Australia
218 Lake Road, Northcote, Auckland, New Zealand

ISBN 978 1 84773 345 0

Editorial Direction: Rosemary Wilkinson
Publisher: Aruna Vasudevan
Editor: Steffanie Brown
Designers: Elmari Kuyler, Phil Kay
Cartographers: Genene Hart, Steve Dew
Cover Design: David Etherington
Production: Melanie Dowland

DISCLAIMER
The author and publishers have made every effort to ensure that the information
contained in this book was accurate at the time of going to press.

Reproduction by Pica Digital PTE Ltd, Singapore
Printed and bound by Times Offset (M) Sdn, Malaysia.

2 4 6 8 10 9 7 5 3 1

PHOTOGRAPHIC CREDITS
Front cover, 59 © Schlegelmilch/Corbis; 1 AFP; 2–5 Touchline Photo; 6–7 Photo Access; 8–9
www.travel-ink.co.uk/Dave Saunders; 10 (top) Touchline Photo; 10 (bottom) Photo Access; 11
Touchline Photo; 12 INPRA/Loic Jacob; 13 galloimages/gettyimages.com; 14 (top) The Bridgeman Art
Library/The Stapleton Collection; 14 (bottom) The Bridgeman Art Library/Mark Fiennes; 15 The
Bridgeman Art Library/Bibliotheque Nationale; 18 The Bridgeman Art Library/Archives Charmet; 20
The Bridgeman Art Library/Roger-Viollet, Paris; 21 The Bridgeman Art Library/National Archives
Trust; 22 (top and bottom) Photo Access; 107 galloimages/gettyimages.com

Contents

INTRODUCING FLAGS 8

Flying the flag 10

The history of flags 14

International organizations 22

World map 24

FLAGS OF THE WORLD 26

Europe...26

Western and Southern Asia 60

Eastern and Southeast Asia 76

Australia, New Zealand and Oceania 90

North America, Central America and the Caribbean 108

South America 136

Africa and adjacent islands 148

De facto states..180

Glossary..185

Index 188

INTRODUCING FLAGS

Flags have always had the power to stir the imagination, and poets and writers have been quick to capture this. In 'Childe Harold's Pilgrimage', the 19th-century English Romantic poet Lord Byron celebrates liberty: 'Yet, Freedom! yet thy banner, torn, but flying / Streams like the thunderstorm against the wind'. Byron invests the flag of freedom with the power to fly against the wind, creating an almost mystic image. Another English poet, Alfred, Lord Tennyson, wrote of the flag as the image of dauntless resistance in 'The Defence of Lucknow', which recalls an incident in the Indian uprising of 1857–58: 'Shot thro' the mast or the halyard, but ever we raised thee anew / And ever from the topmost roof our banner of England blew'.

The 'Star-Spangled Banner' became the official anthem of the United States only in 1931 yet stirring lyrics like 'O say, does that star-spangled banner yet wave/O'er the land of the free and the home of the brave?' resound through the consciousness of all Americans and ensure that they hold their flag in extremely high regard.

FLYING THE FLAG

The flags of independent nations are regarded as being of equal status. Where many national flags are displayed, as at the United Nations (UN) headquarters for instance, care is taken to ensure that no flag receives precedence. One way to accomplish this is to arrange the flagstaffs in a circle that has no beginning or end. The national flag always takes precedence over other flags, such as state or corporate flags. When two flags are flown on a podium, the national flag must be on the speaker's right side (the audience's left). In Europe, when three flags are displayed, the national flag is placed at the centre. A line of more than five flags should have a national flag at each end. In many countries, the national flag takes precedence over military colours, the latter being positioned according to the seniority of the regiments represented.

Above The best way to fly a flag is by using a proper flagpole and halyard.
Top Flags of participating nations on display during the 2002 Winter Olympic Games in Salt Lake City (USA).

Proper usage of national flags

International rules on the use of flags are necessarily a generalization, but following them should help to avoid giving offence. Many countries issue guidelines on how their national flag should be displayed, even if they have no laws concerning this. Military forces, in particular, follow strict protocol where their national and regimental flags are concerned.

Flags should not be put to inappropriate use. A flag should never drag on the floor or fall to the ground. A flag used to cover a commemorative plaque prior to its unveiling should not touch the ground when it falls away and, while it may be acceptable to trim a speaker's table with the national flag, it should not be used as a tablecloth or seat cover. Rules may be broken for formal state funerals, but these ceremonies are usually carried out by those well versed in flag protocol, such as a special military squad.

The USA has detailed regulations for the display and handling of the Stars and Stripes, even specifying how it should be folded, and how old flags should be disposed of. Other countries that have legislated the use of their flags include Egypt, Bahrain, Romania, Monaco and Finland. Curiously, the UK has not written into law any regulations concerning its own Union Flag (often called the Union Jack), which, even after the demise of the great British Empire, still flies in various forms around the world.

The central European custom of draping flags or hanging them vertically as an alternative to flying them from a staff contains potential for embarrassment. Hanging involves displaying a flag so the hoist becomes the upper edge, with the field and all its designs turned through 90 degrees from the masthead position.

Simple bicolours and tricolours can change their identity when draped. The flag of Poland, for instance, may be mistaken for that of Indonesia or Monaco, while the Dutch horizontal tricolour becomes the vertical tricolour of France. Because of the potential for confusion, some countries forbid the draping of their national flag, while others produce special versions of their flag that are designed to be draped or hung vertically.

When to fly a flag

Flags are generally flown from sunrise to sunset, although the hours may be specified according to the clock in those countries that lie in far northern and southern latitudes. (In Finland, the official hours for flying the national flag are between 08:00 and sunset, or not later than 21:00.)

In most countries, government departments fly the flag during office hours. No flag should be flown in the dark, so any flag flying after sunset must be illuminated.

Practicalities of flying a flag

When a flag is flown, it is considered to be free to be unfurled by the wind. This suggests outdoor use, but flags are also used indoors, where they may be displayed either draped or secured to show the full extent of the field.

The principal item for flying a flag is the flagpole, also referred to as a flagstaff (there are several towns in the world called Flagstaff) or a mast. (Strictly, masts belong aboard ship, and the expression 'half-mast' dates from early shipboard use of flags.)

A flagstaff may be made of any rigid material resistant to the adverse conditions in which it might be placed, such as rust or rot. The staff may be embedded in the ground or attached to a base so that the staff can be pivoted and lowered for repairs and maintenance, such as replacing the halyard or the truck. Portable flagstaffs are usually attached to a base, such as a heavy timber X-frame with a socket in the centre for receiving the staff, which is able to resist both wind and clumsy treatment.

Some countries decorate their flagstaffs. In Norway, for instance, the staff is usually white, while the finial (the ornament at the top of the staff) is often a simple knob or a spear point. Staffs from which Israel's national flag is flown are often painted blue for one third of the height, and white for the remainder. Flagstaffs in Belarus are usually painted with a form of golden ochre.

PARTS OF A FLAG

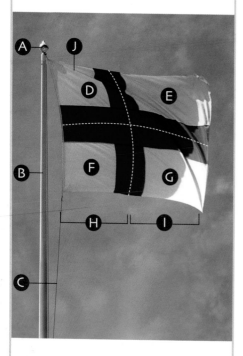

A	finial or ornament	G	lower fly
B	flagpole	H	hoist
C	halyard	I	fly
D	upper hoist	J	canton
E	upper fly		
F	lower hoist		

The size of flag to be flown in any circumstances may be specified by official instructions, but the most important consideration is that it should be impressive in its surroundings. For example, one would not fly a small flag in front of a very large building (unless it is a storm flag in windy conditions).

In a multinational display, flags are usually reduced to the same size, or at least to the same depth (vertical height at the hoist). This means that some flags will not be of the prescribed proportions, but at least it ensures that they are all of approximately the same size.

Flags flown in public should always be in good condition, not torn or faded. They should be easy to hoist and maintain. Some installations include double pulleys and halyards, but a single halyard should be sufficient if it is examined regularly for signs of wear. Most halyards are fitted with a toggle at one end and an eye splice or becket at the other. Some countries have clips on the halyards which attach to grommets in the heading of the flag. A length of rope sewn into the tube, or heading, on the flag's hoist is similarly fitted so that it can be attached to the halyard only when the flag is the right way up. (A flag flown upside down, or in any way but the right way up, is presumed to be a signal of distress.)

Flags used in mourning

Flags are flown at half-mast (half-staff) in mourning for the death of a prominent person, or to indicate a national tragedy. National flags are half-masted only on instructions from the highest authority.

When a flag is to be flown at half-mast it is first raised to its full height and then slowly lowered to the prescribed position. Similarly, before being lowered and removed at the end of the day, a half-masted flag is slowly raised to full height.

At a state or military funeral, the coffin or casket is customarily covered with the deceased person's national flag. The hoist is placed at the head and the top edge draped over the left side of the deceased. The flag is removed before the coffin is placed over the grave and, in the case of US citizens, is ceremonially folded and presented to the next of kin. In an official funeral parade, officers and soldiers generally salute the deceased by dipping their colours as they pass by the casket. The courtesy of carrying a soldier to his grave under his country's flag is sometimes extended to enemy soldiers who die in captivity, or whose bodies are repatriated for burial at home.

There are some variations to half-masting. On days of national mourning in El Salvador, for instance, the flag is flown at half-mast and a length of black crepe is fixed to the top of the staff. In Morocco, to mark mourning on the death of King Hassan II in 1999, the national flag was raised, but was tied so that it could not unfurl. In Spain, mourning is indicated by attaching a piece of black material to the centre of flags that are draped or displayed with the hoist horizontal at the top. A length of black material may be attached to the flagstaff, and the national flag hoisted to half-mast.

Saluting a flag

A flag may be saluted at any time. Uniformed personnel salute according to their unit instructions, while civilians salute according to national custom, by raising a hat, for instance, or standing to attention and facing the flag until it has been raised and broken. Organizations and corporations that fly private or 'house' flags acknowledge them in accordance with their own customs.

Persons in the vicinity of a national flag that is being hoisted should halt and face the flag until it has been raised and broken. 'Breaking' a flag involves hoisting it in a rolled-up state to full height. A tug on the halyard then causes the flag to unfurl or break.

By far the majority of flags are identical on both sides, but it is possible to have a different design on the obverse (the side that is more frequently seen) than the reverse (essentially the secondary side).

As generally depicted in publications, a flag is almost always assumed to have the hoist to the right (reader's left), although some Muslim and other flags have the hoist to the right when the obverse is visible.

Above *When a member of the US armed forces dies in service, the flag used to drape the coffin is ceremonially folded before being presented to the next of kin.*

THE HISTORY OF FLAGS

T he origin of flags lies in the fundamental human need to communicate. When early man roamed the plains and steppes, the waving of a leafy branch could convey essential information if he was beyond voice range, or out of sight of ordinary arm signals. The branch would later have been replaced by a banner of woven reeds, and later still by plain, coarse cloth. Thus a relatively sophisticated system of signalling may have evolved over time.

Humans seek comfort in the company of others who share the same beliefs, and whose numbers offer protection. Ancient examples of rock art show complex associations not only between groups of humans, but with animals, suggesting that clans were known and identified by their totemic figures. Over time, these figures were represented on banners or shields – the forerunners of today's flags.

Above *This herald's tunic depicts the royal lions of England (gold on crimson), Scotland (red on gold), and the harp of Ireland.*
Top *Armour-clad knights used coats of arms to identify themselves to both friend and foe.*

Banners, emblems and coats of arms

Early flags or banners were primarily concerned with identification, so they needed to be readily visible and easily recognized. We imagine that warriors would choose powerful and predatory animals with which to identify themselves, but this was not necessarily so. For instance, the emblem of the Vikings, which aroused terror in those who saw it, was a raven. The 'fatal raven' was consecrated to Odin, the Danish god of war. Legend had it that if defeat lay ahead the raven would droop its wings, but if victory was certain, it adopted a soaring posture, urging its followers on.

Centuries before the Vikings, the Romans chose the eagle as their totem. Cast or sculpted totems, mounted on poles, were carried by the Roman legions that conquered the known world. Emblems and badges evolved more rapidly in military circumstances than in civilian life, because war carried the greater urgency to communicate. By AD100, the Roman infantry marched behind a vexillum, a

Below On the battlefield, flags and banners indicated when soldiers were to advance or retreat.

DECIPHERING A COAT OF ARMS

Above The flags of British-administered territories, and the states of some Commonwealth countries, may show badges or heraldic coats of arms. Top to bottom: South Georgia and the South Sandwich Islands, Western Australia, and Saskatchewan (Canada).
Left Detail from the flag of South Georgia and the South Sandwich islands.

A   Shield – the basic unit of a coat of arms

B   Supporters – figures which hold the shield

C   Crest – the element at the top, above the shield

D   Scroll (bearing a motto) – strip below the shield

E   Compartment – base on which the supporters stand

banner-like flag that was hung from a horizontal rod attached to a long pole. Usually red or purple, it might have been fringed along its lower edge, and often bore the number and symbol of the unit that carried it. 'Vexillology', a word meaning 'the study and collection of information about flags', is derived from the Latin *vexillum*.

The Romans introduced the dragon symbol into Britain (having adopted it from their central Asian enemies). A bronze dragon's head would be fixed to a pole, from which streamed a flag that writhed and curled in the wind like the dragon's tail (much like a modern windsock). Other early flags included the gonfalon with three or more tails, and triangular flags. By the time of the Norman invasion of Britain, most Western flag designs incorporated the

Christian cross, although Harold, the Saxon king who was defeated in 1066, had a banner depicting a dragon, which he may have derived from Welsh tribes he had defeated. The Welsh war leader was traditionally known as Pendragon, or head dragon, and the dragon is still the heraldic symbol of Wales. Dragons also have Biblical associations with Satan (Revelation 12:9) and a great many Christian saints have achieved fame as dragon-slayers.

In the Middle Ages, various devices were used for identification. A knight (a member of the nobility or land-owning class) might choose an emblem by which he could be recognized in battle by his followers. This aid to recognition was needed because, once the visors of their helmets were closed, all knights looked pretty much alike. Let's suppose our knight chose a beaver's head, which he fastened to the crown of his helmet. Let's suppose, too, that he survived a few decades of battle and was able to ride to war with four sturdy sons. They would also wear the beaver's head, but with additional emblems, say an oak leaf or a swan's feather, to distinguish one from the other.

Over time, the emblems by which a knight could be identified on the battlefield were transferred to his shield, while his followers decorated their own shields with a depiction of the emblem which, eventually, became the crest on the knight's coat of arms. It was called a 'coat' of arms because it was displayed not only on the shield, but was also painted or embroidered on the short surcoat the knight wore over his armour. In the 12th and 13th centuries there might be just one or two charges to a shield but, over time, as families expanded through descent and marriage, it required careful study to distinguish one coat of arms from another.

Simplified versions of the coat of arms also began to appear on banners or flags, which had the advantage of being visible from a distance. Clear, bold patterns were essential for quick recognition in the confusion of battle, especially in windless conditions when the flag might droop, or in mist, twilight or at any time that visibility was poor. Foot soldiers, especially, relied on banners and flags to indicate when they should advance or retreat, or where the main thrust of the action was as, unlike mounted knights, they were not able to get a perspective on the battle.

Flags and heraldry

Heraldry is a stylized and standardized way of telling the descent and achievements of an individual, a company, or a country. Coats of arms sometimes appear on flags, and flags on coats of arms. A coat of arms, correctly known as a heraldic achievement, may include a shield 'held' on either side by a supporter (a human or animal figure) standing on a compartment, or base. Above the shield is a crest, usually depicted on top of a metal helmet. There may be one or more scrolls bearing a motto, often in Latin or Medieval French.

An object on the shield, such as a glove, is termed a charge, and the shield is said to be 'charged with a glove'. A charge can be almost anything, including boars' heads, salmon, ships, ears of rye, or even a snake tied into a reef knot. Every object shown is of significance in the history of the family or organization on whose arms it appears.

In heraldry, only a limited range of tinctures – made up of metals and colours – are generally used. The metals are gold (known as or) and silver (argent). When metals are used on flags, or is usually depicted as yellow, and argent as white. The colours of heraldry are red (gules), blue (azure), black (sable), green (vert) and purple (purpure). Purple is rarely used and green is uncommon. Conventional heraldry has no standard colour charts to refer to when an achievement is being described, so gules, for example, may be carmine, vermilion, cerise or maroon.

The same applies to the other tinctures. What matters is that the colour depicted should be unmistakably what it is intended to represent. When a charge is depicted in its natural colours, it is described as proper. This is very

different to the art of creating a modern flag, where the chosen colours are carefully described using international standards of precise shades.

When it comes to flags, heraldic coats of arms or badges are most frequently seen in the flag family of British-administered territories and states. The British Antarctic Territory flag, for example, shows the embellished coat of arms of the Falkland Islands Dependencies – with compartment, mantling (the material draped from the helmet), crest and supporters. By contrast, the flag of Western Australia shows simply the state emblem, or badge, of a black swan on a yellow disc. The flag of the Canadian province of Saskatchewan shows, in addition to a coat of arms, a badge in the form of the western red lily, the province's floral emblem (*see* p16).

Above *Beginning in 1096, crusaders from across Europe set off under the sign of the cross to wrest the Holy Land from the Saracens.*

Crosses and crescents

With the First Crusade (1096–99), Christian leaders from across Europe ceased fighting among themselves for long enough to attempt to carry the cross to the Holy Land – quite literally, as most of them had a large cross painted or embroidered on their surcoat. Each crusading nation had its own colour: red for France and Spain, white for England, blue for Italy, green for Flanders, while the Scots wore the saltire (X-shaped cross) of St Andrew. Although the crusaders' intentions were as varied as the outcome of their missions, a constant aim was to reconquer Palestine from the Muslims (then referred to as Saracens or Moors), with whose flags, symbols and emblems the people of Europe soon became thoroughly acquainted.

Islam prohibits the depiction of living beings, so Muslim imagery tends to feature inscriptions or geometric designs. The crescent was a frequent symbol, although it had been used in central Asia for centuries before the rise of Islam. Some Saracen flags carried an inscription in Arabic: either a religious verse, or a means of identifying a particular leader. The influence on Western heraldry is unclear, but it does appear that the pole with a laterally attached flag was an Arab influence on the West.

A call to arms

Around 1150 heraldry began to develop principles which came to be applied to flags and coats of arms. The number of colours was limited to five and, to ensure optimal visibility at a distance, certain colour combinations were avoided. The use of one colour on another was prohibited unless the

second colour was fimbriated (outlined with one of the metals). Fantastic creatures of legend that found their way into heraldic arms included the dragon, griffin, wyvern and unicorn, while newer motifs included crescents and Saracens' heads, heraldically called Moors' heads. There were several dozen versions of the cross, including the fylfot, the forerunner of the swastika. But designs that were satisfying on a rigid, painted shield did not always transfer successfully to flags.

Persons who were armigerous (entitled to use a coat of arms) were sometimes also entitled to carry a heraldic or armorial banner. Whereas a knight's coat of arms might be identical to his armorial banner, this was rarely the case with the arms of the more nobly born, or of rulers themselves. The royal standard or banner, which gradually evolved as a squarish flag of about 4:5 proportion, frequently had a short fringe in the king's livery or national colours, with one or more decorative tasselled cords in the same colours. An armorial standard or banner could be carried only by the person whose arms were depicted, so other flags, showing personal devices, such as a crest alone, were devised to be carried by his sons or esquires (young men who hoped to become knights themselves).

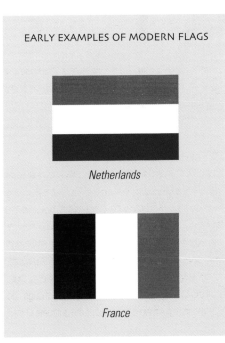

EARLY EXAMPLES OF MODERN FLAGS

Netherlands

France

The evolution of modern flags

By the Middle Ages, royal banners were becoming associated with particular territories, rather than a family or dynasty. Circumstances calling for their display were limited, however, until voyagers began travelling widely and required distinctive flags that could identify their ships. Many early ensigns were armorial (based on a coat of arms), while others featured national colours.

Many countries' flag history begins with an emblem or symbol of their patron saint. England, for example, chose the red cross of St George for a flag, reserving depictions of St George slaying the dragon for other uses. In time, this latter image appeared on coins, medals and patronal banners, while the red cross on a white background remains the flag of England to this day.

The Dutch horizontal tricolour of the 16th century is credited with being the first 'modern' flag, being simple in execution and easy to distinguish, with plain, uncomplicated stripes replacing intricate heraldic devices. It was not long before the orange, white and blue colours were modified for use by the all-powerful Dutch East India Company, through the simple addition of the company's VOC monogram in the white band.

In the late 18th century, two new flags came into being that would resonate as symbols of freedom throughout the western world. Across the Atlantic, the newly independent United States of America asserted itself militarily and symbolically with a novel flag design. It is believed this was the first flag to depict stars, while the colours and pattern were unlike anything that had gone before.

The second notably different flag, that of revolutionary France, used the same red, white and blue colours, but chose three vertical stripes, a pattern that soon became known as the *Tricolore*.

Revolution revisited France in 1848. By that time, the idea of the nation-state, independent and free from the tyranny of monarchy, was igniting a powerful ripple across Europe and South America. Dispensing with the banners and heraldic standards that were the preserve of the elite and the oppressor, ordinary people readily accepted the concept of a national identity, embodied in a common flag,

The right psychological moment, coupled with shrewd stage management, raised one flag and emblem to unprecedented heights of public awareness in the 1930s. This was the flag of Nazi Germany, which revived the red, white and black colours of the former Imperial flag, but arranged them in a crisply modern design. Use of the swastika emblem was actively

Left *The French tricoloured cockade was chosen on 17 July 1789, three days after the storming of the Bastille. Red and blue were the colours of Paris, and white represented the royal house of Bourbon. The first* Tricolore *was authorized on 24 October 1790.*

encouraged on flags, badges, banners and on the huge drapes that festooned buildings in every German town. The flag's career was short, but undoubtedly spectacular.

In South Africa, during the Anglo-Boer War (1899–1902), a light-hearted moment occurred when, in the early phases, Britain suffered a string of humiliating reverses and surrenders. The jubilant Boers joked that the English flag was really a plain white cloth, which was carrying simplistic design too far. In their view, their own republican flags were modern. The Transvaal flew a four-coloured flag comprising a horizontal red, white and blue tricolour, with a vertical green band at the hoist. Their sister republic, the Orange Free State, placed the red, white and blue tricolour in the chief canton, with a field of three orange and four white horizontal stripes.

Above National pride, often embodied by the Stars and Stripes, was a strong motivating force for Americans during World War II.

Symbols of war and peace

Victory and conquest in war, or disapproval of an ousted regime, is sometimes expressed by banning an opponent's flag. Likewise, the burning of a flag, even a representation of it, is frequently associated with conflict.

Throughout history, there have been times when it has been illegal to display, or even possess, certain flags. For instance, during the Nazi occupation of France during World War II, the discovery of a Free French flag with its cross of Lorraine would have had severe consequences. More recently, in the years before the African National Congress legitimately swept to power in South Africa, it was a criminal offence for its flag to be displayed.

Over time, various flags, shields and banners have achieved either fame or notoriety, not so much for their designs or any intrinsic qualities they possessed, but for the events or ideologies with which they were associated. Some are remembered and revered as symbols of good, while others will forever be associated with war or conquest. Very often, the way a particular flag is regarded depends on the personal standpoint of the viewer.

INTERNATIONAL ORGANIZATIONS

H istorically, treaties signed between countries concerned trade concessions or pacts of non-aggression and were often sealed by a marriage between high-ranking partners from either side. Today, the visible seal of approval and acceptance, in place of the marriage, is the joint hoisting of both parties' flags.

At the headquarters of international organizations or associations it is common practice to fly the flag of the host organization in the senior position (first in a line, or at the 12-o'clock position in a circle), together with the national flags of the member states following in alphabetical sequence.

Above The European Union flag maintains 12 stars.
Top Flags outside the European Union headquarters.

United Nations

The UN, founded after the end of World War II, establishes and maintains international peace. The flag, adopted in 1947, has a light blue field on which is a world map within an olive wreath. Both blue and the olive branches symbolize world peace, and the map denotes global concern.

With 192 members, the United Nations is the world's largest and most influential international organization. In times of war, the UN may send soldiers and military equipment to the trouble zone, but the troops may engage only in self-defence and are primarily peacekeepers.

European Union

In 1955, the Council of Europe adopted a flag with a circle of gold stars at the centre. The design was adopted by the Council's successor, the European Union (EU), in May 1986. Originally, the intent was to show one star for each member nation, but it was finally decided to have an arbitrary number of stars on the flag.

Commonwealth

Before World War I, the British Empire commanded over 25 per cent of the world's population and area. With the fall of many European thrones, the term 'British Commonwealth of Nations' came to represent the remaining empire, but was soon simplified to the Commonwealth. A voluntary association of countries, colonies or territories that were, or are still, ruled by Britain, the Commonwealth today includes some 53 states from across the world. The annual Commonwealth Heads of Government meeting is an important forum for discussions on global issues. The flag has a dark blue field with a globe, upon which no countries are depicted. The globe emits short gold lines, with a gap, to form the letter C.

Association of Southeast Asian Nations

The flag was adopted in 1997, 30 years after the ASEAN was founded to promote economic cooperation and stability among the states of Southeast Asia. Red, white, blue and gold are the colours of the member states. The blue field represents sea, sky and friendship, and the central emblem, on a red disc outlined in white, represents 10 padi stalks, one for each member nation.

Red Cross, Red Crescent and Red Crystal

A red cross couped on a white field has been the symbol of the International Committee of the Red Cross since the humanitarian organization was founded in 1863. The Red Cross concerns itself with human welfare in times of war, natural disaster, or humanitarian crisis. It has also played a role in successive Geneva Conventions on the conduct of war and the treatment of prisoners of war. An equivalent flag for use in Muslim countries displays a red crescent and was adopted in 1876. The red crystal flag is sometimes used as a neutral emblem by those states objecting to the cross or crescent on religious grounds.

FLAGS OF SOME INTERNATIONAL ORGANIZATIONS

United Nations   Red Cross   Red Crescent   Red Crystal   Association of Southeast Asian Nations   Commonwealth

World map

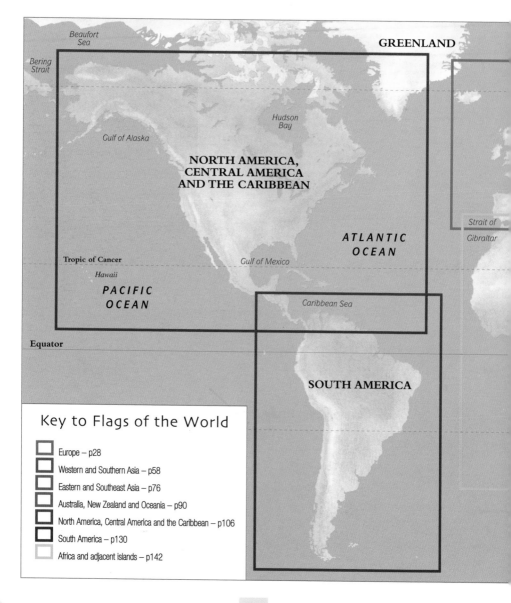

Beaufort
Sea

GREENLAND

Bering
Strait

Hudson
Bay

Gulf of Alaska

**NORTH AMERICA,
CENTRAL AMERICA
AND THE CARIBBEAN**

*ATLANTIC
OCEAN*

Strait of

Gibraltar

Tropic of Cancer

Gulf of Mexico

Hawaii

*PACIFIC
OCEAN*

Caribbean Sea

Equator

SOUTH AMERICA

Key to Flags of the World

- Europe – p28
- Western and Southern Asia – p58
- Eastern and Southeast Asia – p76
- Australia, New Zealand and Oceania – p90
- North America, Central America and the Caribbean – p106
- South America – p130
- Africa and adjacent islands – p142

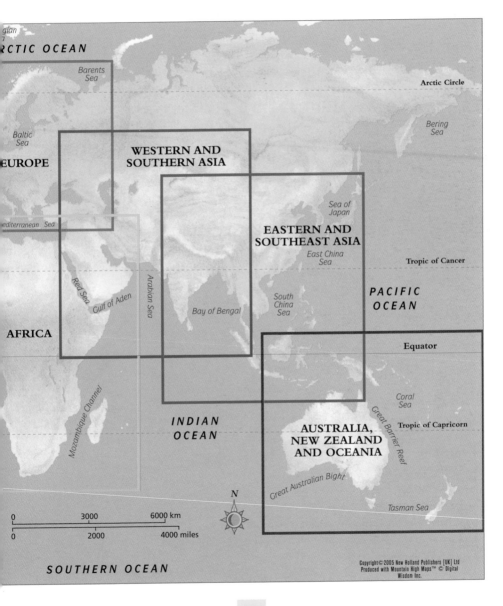

gian

EUROPE

From Portugal's Atlantic coastline to Russia's Ural Mountains, and from Norway's remote North Cape to the Mediterranean island of Crete, the 'Old World' of Europe presents a tight pattern of settlement. For centuries, the focal point of cultural and trade development in Europe was the Mediterranean. Later, shore settlements along the Atlantic and North Sea coastlines played a greater role. From city-states and unsteady kingdoms, 15th-century explorers set out in their fragile craft to find a sea route to the east. They found a New World, and the culture the European colonists carried and imparted wherever they went has profoundly influenced the world ever since.

In the early centuries, despite the proximity of borders, there was little friendly contact between nations. There were occasional instances of collaboration, such as the Crusades of the 11th and 12th centuries. However, for the most part treaties kept an uneasy peace. Twentieth-century political alliances and politics, transformed into two World Wars, brought about the destruction of long-ruling dynasties, which saw the rise of Communism. Following its fall in the 1990s, Sarajevo came to the fore as a city besieged by Christian Serbs indulging in a bloody 'ethnic cleansing' of Muslims. UN, NATO and Russian troops brought a temporary lull but, in the Caucasus to the east, Russian troops launched an attack on the would-be independent republic of Chechnya. The UN and European Union (EU) attempted to mediate, producing an uneasy peace that was sporadically and viciously broken.

Although the EU counts as members almost all the states of western Europe, as well as some in central Europe, the European Parliament has still to overcome the suspicions of national parliaments and has not yet fully established itself.

AT A GLANCE

Largest country: Russia
Smallest country: Vatican City
Largest city: Moscow (Russian Federation)
Major cities: Athens, Barcelona, Berlin, Birmingham, Budapest, Geneva, Hamburg, Istanbul, Kiev, London, Madrid, Manchester, Milan, Naples, Paris, Rome, St Petersburg, Warsaw.

Highest point: Mt Elbrus (Elbruz), Caucasus – 5,642m (18,517ft) – the highest point in Western Europe.
Lowest point: Caspian Sea shore – 28m (92ft) below sea level.
Longest rivers: Volga, European Russia – 3,530km (2,193mi).
Largest lake: Caspian Sea – 371,000km^2 (142,200sq mi).

Europe

Barents Sea

Arctic Circle

Beloye More
[White Sea]

AND

RUSSIA

sinki
nn
ONIA

TVIA
a
IUANIA

Moscow

BELARUS
Minsk

Kiev

KRAINE

Caspian Sea

DNIESTER
REPUBLIC

MOLDOVA
Chisinau   Tiraspol

Mt Elbrus   SOUTH
5642m   OSSETIA
(18517ft)   Tskhinvali   Baki

ABKHAZIA   AZERBAIJAN
ROMANIA   Suchumi   T'Bilisi
ade   Bucharest   Black Sea   GEORGIA   Stepanakert
                                         ARMENIA
BULGARIA   Yerevan   KARABAKH

Sofia
pje
ONIA   Ankara   TURKEY

ECE

Athens
                    NORTHERN
                    CYPRUS
Aegean Sea   Nicosia
Crete   CYPRUS

UNITED KINGDOM

United Kingdom of Great Britain and Northern Ireland

Flag proportions: 1:2
Adopted: 1 January 1801
Capital: London
Area: 244,088km² (94,242sq mi)
Population: 60,588,000
Language: English

Religion: Non-religious, Church of England, Roman Catholic
Currency: Pound sterling
Exports: Electrical equipment, road vehicles, petroleum.

The Union Flag's origins date to 1277 when the banner of England's patron saint, St George (a red cross quartering a white field), was sometimes used as the flag of England. The white diagonal cross of St Andrew of Scotland dates back to at least 1385. Following the accession of James VI of Scotland to the throne of England, he chose a combined flag in 1606 for use as a jack on naval vessels, hence the origin of the name 'Union Jack'.

No change was made to it when England and Scotland formed the United Kingdom of Great Britain. The 1801 Act of Union founded the United Kingdom of Great Britain and Ireland. St Patrick's cross (a red saltire) was added as a counterchange to St Andrew's cross, forming the present flag.

IRELAND

Eire (Republic of Ireland)

Flag proportions: 1:2
Adopted: 29 December 1937
Capital: Dublin (Baile Átha Cliath)
Area: 70,285km² (27,137sq mi)
Population: 4,240,000
Language: English, Irish

Religion: Roman Catholic
Currency: Euro
Exports: Machinery and transport equipment, computers, chemical products and pharmaceuticals, live animals, food products.

The 1916 Easter Rising, a rebellion against British rule, led to the formation of the Irish Free State in 1922, followed by independence in 1937. A green, white and orange tricolour was raised as the national flag of the Irish Free State (known after 1949 as the Republic of Ireland). The colours were worn in cockades in sympathy with a French uprising that led to the restoration of the *Tricolore*, and also used by Irish nationalists in their 1848 struggle for freedom from Britain. Green represents the Catholic majority, orange the Protestant minority, and white expresses union and peace between the two faiths.

GUERNSEY

The Bailiwick of Guernsey

Flag proportions: 1:2
Adopted: 30 April 1985
Capital: St Peter Port
Area: 78.5km² (30sq mi)
Population: 62,700
Language: English

Religion: Anglican, Roman Catholic
Currency: Local issue of UK pound
Exports: Tomatoes, cut flowers, vegetables, dairy produce, cattle.

Guernsey, with its smaller dependencies of Alderney and Sark (which have their own flags), lies west of Normandy. The coasts of all three islands are lined by cliffs. The island, which once depended upon tourism and farming, is now a financial services centre. The flag of Guernsey, which is modern in origin, is white with a red cross, upon which is superimposed a smaller shortened gold cross with triangular arms.

JERSEY

The Bailiwick of Jersey

Flag proportions: 1:2
Adopted: 7 April 1981
Capital: St Helier
Area: 116km² (45sq mi)
Population: 87,200
Language: English
Religion: Anglican,

Roman Catholic
Currency: Local issue of UK pound
Exports: Light industrial goods, flowers, potatoes, tomatoes, dairy products.

Jersey, which lies 19 km (12 miles) west of the French Cotentin peninsula, is, along with Guernsey, all that is left to the British crown of the Duchy of Normandy. The island, which now depends upon financial services, did not have its own flag until modern times. The flag of Jersey is white with a red saltire (diagonal cross), above which are the arms of the island, a gold crown above three lions on a red shield.

ISLE OF MAN

Isle of Man

Flag proportions: 2:5
Adopted: August 1971 (officially; used since 13th century)
Capital: Douglas
Area: 572km² (221sq mi)
Population: 80,100

Language: English
Religion: Anglican
Currency: Local issue of UK pound
Exports: Tweed cloth, fish and shellfish, meat.

Formerly a separate kingdom, the Isle of Man, which lies in the Irish Sea between northwest England and Northern Ireland, came under English control in the fourteenth century, but, like the Channel Islands, it is not part of the United Kingdom. The island's flag is red with a three-legged symbol, known as a trinacria, at the centre. This symbol is thought to be of Norse origin and also occurs in Sicily, which was once a Norman kingdom.

PORTUGAL

Portuguese Republic

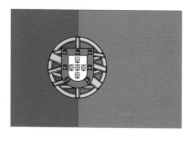

Flag proportions: 2:3
Adopted: 30 June 1911
Capital: Lisbon (Lisboa)
Area: 92,391km² (35,672sq mi)
Population: 10,570,000
Language: Portuguese

Religion: Roman Catholic
Currency: Euro
Exports: Textiles, clothing, footwear, machinery and transport equipment, chemicals, paper products, cork.

Portugal's lead in exploring the world beyond Europe in the 15th and 16th centuries is reflected in the armillary sphere, an old navigation instrument, depicted on the flag. The original shield of Portugal, from the reign of Alfonso Henriques in the 12th century, was white with five blue shields in the form of a cross, representing five Moorish kings defeated in battle in 1139. On each shield, five white dots represent the wounds of Christ. The red border with gold castles was added in the 13th century by King Alfonso III. The red field was adopted to signify revolution, while green depicted the colour of hope.

SPAIN

The Kingdom of Spain

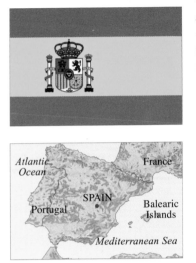

Flag proportions: 2:3
Adopted: 24 December 1981
Capital: Madrid
Area: 504,782km²
(194,897sq mi)
Population: 45,201,000
Language: Spanish (Castalian),
Catalan, Galician (Gallego),
Basque
Religion: Roman Catholic
Currency: Euro
Exports: Machinery and transport
equipment, agricultural products,
machinery.

Red and yellow appeared on Catalonia's flag in the 13th century, and on other provincial flags, notably Castile and Aragon. These colours were used from 1785 to identify Spanish merchant shipping. A purple band was added when Spain became a republic in 1931, but the original flag was restored in 1939. Since then, the state flag has incorporated the national arms, in the yellow band. The quarters of the shield represent four regions of Spain: Castile, León, Aragon and Navarre. The shield is supported by the Pillars of Hercules, as Gibraltar and Jebel Musa were once known. The arms have changed many times, the last being in 1981.

GIBRALTAR

Gibraltar

Flag proportions: 1:2
Adopted: 1983
Capital: Gibraltar
Area: 6.5km² (2.5sq mi)
Population: 27,500
Language: English
Religion: Roman Catholic
Currency: Gibraltar Pound
Exports: Re-exported petroleum,
machinery, manufactured goods.

The unofficial flag shows a three-towered castle and golden key on a white field with a red band at the base. The arms, granted in 1502 by Spain's King Ferdinand, also feature a castle and key, symbolizing the security of Gibraltar and its control of access to the Mediterranean through the Straits of Gibraltar.

Gibraltar has been under British control since 1713, yet Spain continues to claim sovereignty, despite referendums in favour of maintaining the status quo.

ANDORRA

Principality of Andorra

Flag proportions: 2:3
Adopted: July 1993
Capital: Andorra la Vella
Area: 468km² (181sq mi)
Population: 81,200
Language: Catalan,

Spanish (Castilian)
Religion: Roman Catholic
Currency: Euro
Industries: Tobacco products,
furniture, clothing, newspapers
and periodicals.

The Principality of Andorra is one of the world's oldest states. Its flag dates from around 1897, but its origin and symbolism are not documented. France and Spain have protected Andorra since the 13th century, and are represented by red and yellow (Spain) and blue and red (France).

The arms represent Spain's bishop of Urgel and the French Comte de Foix, under whose joint sovereignty Andorra was placed in 1278. The joint heads of state are still the bishop of Urgel and the president of France, represented by permanent delegates. Elements on the coat of arms recall Catalonia and Béarn on which, historically, Andorra has been dependent.

FRANCE

French Republic

Flag proportions: 2:3
Adopted: 5 March 1848
Capital: Paris
Area: 547,030km²
(211, 208sq mi), metropolitan
France, excluding overseas
départemements and territories

Population: 60,825,000
Language: French
Religion: Roman Catholic
Currency: Euro
Exports: Machinery and transport
equipment, aircraft, plastics, iron,
steel, chemical products.

France's national flag, the *Tricolore*, has been in uninterrupted use since 1848. Blue and red are generally accepted as the colours of Paris. White, the colour of the royal House of Bourbon, is also associated with the Virgin Mary and the 15th-century French heroine, Jeanne d'Arc. The colours represent the ideals of the 1789 French Revolution: liberty, equality and fraternity.

The *Tricolore* is flown with blue at the hoist. The *Tricolore* is the official flag of France's Overseas Territories (such as Réunion and French Polynesia), some of which fly approved local flags alongside it.

MONACO

Principality of Monaco

Flag proportions: 4:5
Adopted: 4 April 1881
Capital: Monaco-Ville
Area: 2km² (3/4sq mi)
Population: 32,000
Language: French, Italian,

Monegasque
Religion: Roman Catholic
Currency: Euro
Exports: Chemicals, plastics,
electronic and consumer goods.

Monaco, the second smallest state in the world, forms an enclave in southern France. The steep territory is gradually being expanded by filling in the sea to reclaim more land. The flag, equal bands of red over white, takes its colours from the arms of the Grimaldi family, who have ruled the principality for over 700 years. Monaco's flag is the same as the Indonesian bicolour, differing only in proportion.

BELGIUM

Kingdom of Belgium

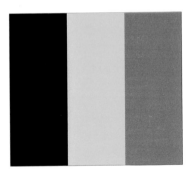

Flag proportions: 13:15
Adopted: 23 January 1831
Capital: Brussels (Bruxelles)
(Brussel)
Area: 30,528km² (11,787sq mi)
Population: 10,585,000
Languages: Dutch (Flemish),
French

Religion: Roman Catholic
Currency: Euro
Exports: Machinery and transport equipment, chemicals (particularly plastics), diamonds, metals (particularly iron and steel), food, textiles.

Belgium is a parliamentary democracy with a constitutional monarch. The vertical tricolour was almost certainly based on the French *Tricolore* and came into use with the founding of the independent Kingdom of Belgium in 1830. The colours appeared on the coat of arms of the Duchy of Brabant, a large province of the Low Countries (an area that encompassed Belgium, the Netherlands and Luxembourg).

The original arms of Brabant featured a gold lion rampant, its tongue and claws red, on a black field. A lion on a shield still features on the Belgian coat of arms.

LUXEMBOURG
Grand Duchy of Luxembourg

Flag proportions: 3:5
Adopted: 1848
Capital: Luxembourg
Area: 2,586km² (999sq mi)
Population: 452,000
Languages: Letzebuergesch,

German, French
Religion: Roman Catholic
Currency: Euro
Exports: Machinery and transport
equipment, steel, chemicals,
rubber, glass, processed food.

The horizontal tricolour of Luxembourg, Europe's last independent duchy, derived its colours from the 13th-century arms of the Grand Duke. Luxembourg was part of the Netherlands in the early 19th century, so the pattern and colours of the two flags are similar, although Luxembourg has a paler shade of blue. In the mid-20th century, Luxembourg formed an economic union with Belgium and the Netherlands (Benelux), setting the scene for the establishment of the European Union.

THE NETHERLANDS
Kingdom of the Netherlands

Flag proportions: 2:3
Adopted: 19 February 1937
Capital: Amsterdam (capital in
name only); The Hague (legislative
and administrative capital)
Area: 41,526km² (16,033sq mi)
Population: 16,358,000
Language: Dutch

Religion: Non-religious, Roman
Catholic, Dutch Reformed,
Calvinist
Currency: Euro
Exports: Machinery and transport
equipment, chemicals and
chemical products, petroleum,
foodstuffs, electrical goods.

The first horizontal tricolour of The Netherlands, known as the Prinsenvlag, was raised in the 16th century. It had an orange band in honour of William the Silent, the protestant Prince of Orange, who rebelled against the Catholic Philip II of Spain, establishing an independent country in 1581. Red gradually replaced orange and, by the 18th century, was the confirmed colour.

Orange remains the Dutch royal colour and, on festive days connected to the royal family, an orange pennant is hoisted above the national flag.

DENMARK
Kingdom of Denmark

Flag proportions: 28:37
Adopted: 1625
Capital: Copenhagen (København)
Area: 43,094km² (16,639sq mi) 'metropolitan' Denmark, excluding dependencies
Population: 5,447,000

Language: Danish
Religion: Evangelical Lutheran
Currency: Danish Krone
Exports: Machinery and equipment, pig meat and meat products, dairy products, fish, pharmaceuticals and chemicals.

The Kingdom of Denmark dates from the 10th century, and the *Dannebrog* is often claimed to be the oldest national flag. Although it can be officially dated to the second half of the 14th century, legend says that a vision of a white cross on a red field came to King Valdemar II during a crusade against the pagan Estonians in 1219. Spurred on by this sign, the Danes went on to win the battle. It was not until 1854 that private people were allowed to fly the flag.

The off-centre cross was originally a conventional square-armed cross, but was amended so that its arm in the fly was extended. It is the model for the flags of all Scandinavian countries.

THE FAEROES
Faeroe Islands

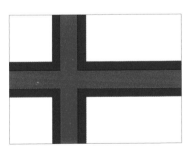

Flag proportions: 8:11
Adopted: 5 June 1959
Capital: Tórshavn
Area: 1399km² (540sq mi)
Population: 48,400
Languages: Faeroese, Danish

Religion: Evangelical Lutheran, Plymouth Brethren
Currency: Danish Krone
Exports: Fish and fish products, boats, postage stamps.

The people of the Faeroe Islands are descended from Viking settlers who arrived in the 9th century. The archipelago of 17 inhabited islands and one uninhabited island has been connected to Denmark since the 14th century and became a self-governing overseas administrative division in 1948.

Set on a white field, a red cross is narrowly bordered in blue. Blue and red occur in traditional Faeroese headdresses, while white represents sky, and waves breaking against the coast. The first flag was only used on land, but during World War II it became the ensign of the British-occupied Faeroes so as to distinguish their ships from those of German-occupied Denmark.

ICELAND

The Republic of Iceland

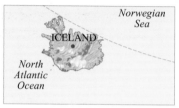

Flag proportions: 18:25
Adopted: 17 June 1944
Capital: Reykjavík
Area: 102,819km²
(39,699sq mi)
Population: 307,000

Language: Icelandic
Religion: Evangelical Lutheran
Currency: Icelandic Krona
Exports: Frozen fish, shrimps
lobsters, salted fish, fresh fish,
aluminium, doatomite.

Iceland's traditional colours are blue and white, for the sea and the ice. The flag shows a white horizontal cross on a blue field. To this was added red, the combination depicting a historical connection to Norway, from which many Icelanders' ancestors come.

Iceland was under Danish occupation and influence from the 14th century and, from the 16th century, was represented in the arms of Denmark by, among other charges or objects, a stockfish crowned. The state flag depicts the national arms on a swallow-tailed flag.

NORWAY

Kingdom of Norway

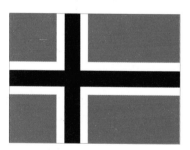

Flag proportions: 8:11
Adopted: 17 July 1821
Capital: Oslo
Area: 323,878km²
(125,050sq mi)
Population: 4,681,000
Language: Norwegian (Bokmaal
and Nynorsk or Landsmaal)

Religion: Evangelical Lutheran,
Russian Orthodox
Currency: Norwegian Krone
Exports: Petroleum and natural
gas and their products, machinery
and transport equipment, metals
and metal products, chemicals,
ships, fish and fish products.

Norway was ruled by Denmark from 1380, during which time Norwegian ships flew the Dannebrog. The country was ceded to Sweden in 1814 and the current flag dates from 1821, when a member of the Norwegian parliament, Frederik Meltzer, suggested charging the Danish flag with a blue cross. Red, white and blue are the colours of the French revolutionary *Tricolore* and the flags of the USA and UK. In 1899, after a long struggle, Norway obtained the right to fly its flag without the 'union badge'. After gaining independence in 1905, Norway retained that flag which is often flown from white-painted poles, usually with a spike or ball terminal.

SVALBARD

Svalbard

Flag proportions: 8:11
Adopted: n/a
Capital: Longyearbyen
Area: 62,703km²
(24,273 sq mi)
Population: 2,500

Languages: Norwegian, Russian
Religion: Evangelical Lutheran
(Church of Norway), Russian
Orthodox
Currency: Norwegian Krone
Exports: Coal, furs.

Svalbard is a bleak Arctic archipelago, some 60 per cent of which is covered by ice. Only Spitsbergen's western fjord coast is ice-free all year. The status of Svalbard, sometimes called Spitsbergen for its largest island, was disputed until 1920, when a treaty signed by 41 nations gave sovereignty to Norway and equal rights to minerals (largely coal) on the islands to the signatories. Only Norway and Russia mine on Svalbard, however. All settlements on Svalbard are coal-mining towns. Svalbard uses the flag of Norway.

SWEDEN

Kingdom of Sweden

Flag proportions: 5:8
Adopted: 22 June 1906
Capital: Stockholm
Area: 449,964km²
(173,806sq mi)
Population: 9,113,000
Language: Swedish

Religion: Lutheran (Church of
Sweden), non-religious
Currency: Swedish Krona
Exports: Machinery and transport
equipment, paper products and
wood, chemicals, iron and steel
products.

A royal decree of 1569 commanded that Swedish battle flags were to depict a gold or yellow cross. The design of the national flag, a horizontal gold cross on a blue field, dates from soon after. The colours come from the national coat of arms, which originated in the 14th century.

The arms consist of a blue shield quartered by a gold cross. Three gold crowns are depicted in the first and fourth quarters, and a lion in the second and third quarters. The shield is supported by two gold lions.

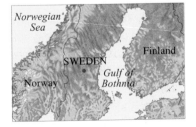

FINLAND

Republic of Finland

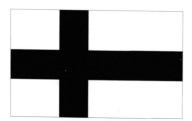

Flag proportions: 11:18
Adopted: 1 January 1995
Capital: Helsinki (Helsingfors)
Area: 336,618km² (129,969sq mi), excluding the Aland Islands
Population: 5,250,000
Languages: Finnish, Swedish

Religion: Evangelical Lutheran
Currency: Euro
Exports: Machinery, chemicals, metal products, timber, paper and paper products, telecommunications equipment.

White is for the snow, and blue for the skies and this country's many lakes. Finland proclaimed its independence from Russia in 1917 and was recognized in 1920. Although its flag was introduced in 1918, various combinations of blue and white had featured on Finnish flags for hundreds of years. Use of the flag is regulated by law, with the hours for flying it being from 08:00 to sunset, or 21:00 at the latest. Helsinki, Europe's northernmost capital, lies only some six degrees south of the Arctic Circle, but does not experience the midnight sun phenomenon.

The state flag and ensign carry the Finnish arms' motif, a lion rampant bearing a sword, on a red field, at the junction of the arms of the cross.

ALAND

Åland

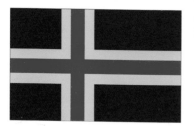

Flag proportions: 3:4
Adopted: 1954
Capital: Mariehamn
Area: 1,527km² (590sq mi)
Population: 26,900

Language: Swedish
Religion: Evangelical Lutheran
Currency: Euro
Exports: Foodstuffs, re-exported consumer goods.

The Aland Islands, which had been Swedish since the twelfth century, were ceded to Russia in 1809 and incorporated into Russian-ruled Finland. When Finland gained independence in 1917, the islands attempted to secede and rejoin Sweden. In 1921, international agreement established the islands as a self-governing, neutral Finnish territory. The flag of Aland is that of Sweden, with the addition of a red cross superimposed on the gold cross.

ESTONIA
Republic of Estonia

Flag proportions: 7:11
Adopted: 8 May 1990
Capital: Tallinn
Area: 45,227km² (17,462sq mi)
Population: 1,342,000
Language: Estonian, Russian
Religion: Non-religious, Estonian

Orthodox, Lutheran
Currency: Kroon
Exports: Machinery, wood and wood products (including paper), textiles and clothing, foodstuffs (particularly dairy products) metals, chemicals.

A former Baltic province of imperial Russia, Estonia raised its flag of independence in 1918 after the Russians made peace with Germany. The horizontal tricolour of blue over black over white represent Estonian folklore: blue for sky, faith and loyalty; black to commemorate a past of suffering, as well as the soil; and white for snow and for hope. When Soviet Russia occupied Estonia during World War II, the tricolour was banned. From 1987–88, when communism was failing, the flag was openly displayed and it became the national flag of the Republic of Estonia in 1990.

Three gold lions on the coat of arms represent three eras of heroic struggle: in ancient times, during the 14th century and in the 20th century.

LATVIA
Republic of Latvia

Flag proportions: 1:2
Adopted: 27 February 1990
Capital: Riga
Area: 64,610km² (24,945sq mi)
Population: 2,281,000
Language: Latvian (also known as Lettish), Russian

Religion: Non-religious, Lutheran, Roman Catholic
Currency: Lat
Exports: Timber and paper products, machinery and transport equipment, metals, textiles, food and agricultural products.

This flag's colours are unique to Latvia. There is some evidence that, in the 13th century, Latvian clans used a flag of somewhat similar design. The modern version, based on an old written document, was developed and used in the late 19th century and also from 1918–40, when Latvia was independent. Red is for the past blood shed and white for truth, right and honour. Use of the flag was banned under Soviet rule, which commenced in 1940, but resumed when Latvia gained independence in 1990.

The arms of Latvia feature a griffin, a mythical winged beast representing a combination of strength and swiftness.

LITHUANIA
Republic of Lithuania

Flag proportions: 1:2
Adopted: 20 March 1989
Capital: Vilnius
Area: 65,301km² (25,213sq mi)
Population: 3,385,000
Language: Lithuanian

Religion: Roman Catholic
Currency: Litas
Exports: Mineral products, textiles and clothing, machinery and equipment, chemicals, wood and wood products, foodstuffs.

Once Lithuania was free from Russian rule after World War I, it adopted the present flag, a horizontal tricolour of yellow above green above red. Reoccupation by Russia in 1940 resulted in the flag being suppressed until full independence was gained in 1991. Yellow represents ripening wheat with its promise of freedom from hunger, green is for the country's forests and for hope, and red symbolizes courage in the cause of patriotism.

POLAND
The Republic of Poland

Flag proportions: 5:8
Adopted: 1 August 1919
Capital: Warsaw (Warszawa)
Area: 312,685km² (120,628sq mi)
Population: 38,132,000
Language: Polish
Religion: Roman Catholic

Currency: Zloty
Exports: Manufactured goods, machinery and transport equipment, consumer goods, foodstuffs (particularly poultry, eggs, pork, fruit and vegetables).

This flag has horizontal bands of white over red, while the civil ensign and diplomatic flag have a red shield at their centre. The use of red and white dates from the 13th century, but became the national colours only in 1831.

The national arms are said to date from 1228. They depict a white eagle, crowned, on a red field, and have remained relatively constant despite a troubled history that saw Poland partitioned among Prussia, Russia and Austria. The eagle also retained its crown long after the fall of the Polish monarchy, although the crown was removed under communist rule (1945–89) and restored only after the fall of communism.

CZECH REPUBLIC

Czech Republic

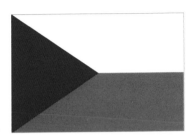

Flag proportions: 2:3
Adopted: 30 March 1920
Capital: Prague (Praha)
Area: 78,864km² (30,450sq mi)
Population: 10,287,000
Language: Czech
Religion: Non-religious,

Roman Catholic
Currency: Koruna
Exports: Manufactured goods,
industrial machinery, motor
vehicles, chemicals, raw
materials, fuel.

With the creation of Czechoslovakia in 1918, after the break-up of the Austro-Hungarian Empire following World War I, a blue isosceles triangle was added to the hoist to distinguish the flag from that of Poland. Czechoslovakia comprised Bohemia, Moravia and part of Silesia, with Slovakia, formerly part of Hungary. After the country was occupied by Germany in 1939, the flag was banned, and restored only in 1945 just before the communists came to power. When the Czech Republic and Slovakia separated in 1993, the Czechs retained the original flag, with its elements of the past. Red and white are derived from the emblem of Bohemia (a silver or white lion on a red field), while blue represents the state of Moravia.

GERMANY

The Federal Republic of Germany

Flag proportions: 3:5
Adopted: 23 May 1949
Capital: Berlin
Area: 357,021km²
(137,846sq mi)
Population: 82,315,000
Language: German

Religion: Evangelical Lutheran,
Roman Catholic
Currency: Euro
Exports: Machinery, road
transport vehicles and equipment,
chemicals and chemical products,
metals, foodstuffs, textiles.

The black-red-gold flag was adopted in 1848 for the anticipated union of German states. When the German Empire came into being in 1871, black, white and red were chosen. The black-red-gold flag was restored by the Weimar Republic. When the National Socialist (Nazi) Party came into power in 1933, it reverted to red, white and black as the national colours, and decreed that the party flag should be the national flag. After World War II, the Weimar tricolour became the flag of the Federal Republic of Germany. From 1949–90, West Germany was made up of 11 states. Since reunification with East Germany this has increased to 16, each with its own state and/or civil flags.

SWITZERLAND

Swiss Confederation

Flag proportions: 1:1
Adopted: 12 December 1889
Capital: Berne (Bern)
Area: 41,285km² (15,940sq mi)
Population: 7,461,000
Languages: German, French, Italian, Romansch

Religion: Roman Catholic, Calvinist, Evangelical Lutheran
Currency: Swiss franc
Exports: Machinery and electronics, chemical and pharmaceutical products, metals, precision instruments.

A white upright cross couped (cut short) on a red field is a relic of medieval times, when many European states flew a cross on a plain field. In the 13th century, the Schwyz canton used a white cross on a red field, and this may have influenced the choice of flag for the confederation of Swiss cantons. The national flag was introduced in 1848 as military colours and the proportions were regulated in 1852. The flag represents neutrality and refuge.

The flags of all 26 Swiss cantons originate from armorial banners based on the arms of the cantons, many of which date from the 14th and 15th centuries.

LIECHTENSTEIN

Principality of Liechtenstein

Flag proportions: 3:5
Adopted: 18 September 1982
Capital: Vaduz
Area: 160km² (62sq mi)
Population: 35,000
Language: German

Religion: Roman Catholic
Currency: Swiss franc
Exports: Audio and video connectors, electronics and precision instruments, dental products and hardware, foodstuffs.

Liechtenstein was a Principality of the Holy Roman Empire in 1719. It has been independent since 1806. At the 1936 Berlin Olympic Games it was discovered that Haiti and Liechtenstein's flags were identical, so in the following year a gold crown was placed in the chief canton of the Liechtenstein flag. There are two versions of the national flag, with the crown placed so as to be upright whether the flag is flown in the usual way or hung vertically.

Blue depicts clear skies, red, embers in the hearth, and gold signifies that the people and the princely house are united in heart and soul. The Prince of Liechtenstein carries his coat of arms on the national flag.

AUSTRIA
Republic of Austria

Flag proportions: 2:3
Adopted: 1 May 1945
Capital: Vienna (Wien)
Area: 83,858km² (32,378sq mi)
Population: 8,299,000
Language: German

Religion: Roman Catholic
Currency: Euro
Exports: Machinery and transport equipment (particularly motor vehicles), paper and paperboard, chemicals, metal goods.

The Austro-Hungarian Empire was one of many monarchies that disappeared in the wake of World War I, but the new republic retained a simple red-white-red tribar dating from at least 1230. According to legend, an Austrian duke was once involved in a battle in which his surcoat became liberally splashed with blood. When he removed his sword belt a white band was seen, and this honourable emblem became the basis of the national flag. Austria is divided into nine states, each with its own flag.

The state flag is charged with a black heraldic eagle holding a hammer in one claw and a sickle in the other.

ITALY
The Republic of Italy

Flag proportions: 2:3
Adopted: 18 June 1946
Capital: Rome (Roma)
Area: 301,277km² (116,324sq mi)
Population: 56,131,000
Language: Italian

Religion: Roman Catholic
Currency: Euro
Exports: Engineering products, textiles and clothing, production machinery, motor vehicles and other transport equipment, chemicals, foodstuffs.

A collection of city-republics, kingdoms and papal states, Italy was temporarily united under French rule from 1796–1814, during which time the Italian tricolour was designed, reputedly by Napoleon. In 1861, when Victor Emmanuel II formed the Kingdom of Italy, the colours were retained, with the coat of arms of the House of Savoy added to the centre of the flag. The arms were removed in 1946 when Italy became a republic.

The Italian civil ensign carries a quartered shield bearing the emblems of Venice (the winged lion of St Mark), Genoa (St George's cross), Amalfi (Maltese cross) and Pisa (Pisan cross).

SAN MARINO

The Most Serene Republic
of San Marino

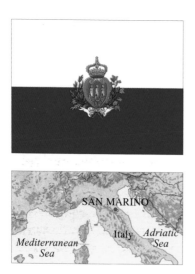

Flag proportions: 4:5
Adopted: 6 April 1862
Capital: San Marino
Area: 61km² (24sq mi)
Population: 30,400
Language: Italian

Religion: Roman Catholic
Currency: Euro
Exports: Building stone, wine, cheese, wood, chestnuts, ceramics.

The Republic of San Marino is one of the oldest and smallest states in the world. Although the country dates from the 4th century, the flag was devised only in 1797. It comprises two equal horizontal bands (white over blue). White represents peace and the clouds surrounding Mount Titano, on which San Marino is built, while blue is for liberty and the sky. Although San Marino is a republic, the arms feature a crown, a symbol of independence. They also depict three white towers on a blue field, each tower on the summit of a peak, and each with an ostrich plume rising from the top. The arms are placed at the centre of the flag for official purposes only.

VATICAN CITY

The State of the Vatican City
(also known as The Holy See)

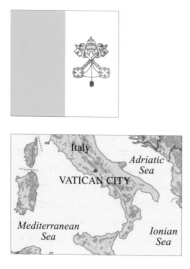

Flag proportions: 1:1
Adopted: 22 February 2001
Capital: Vatican City
Area: 0.44km² (3/20sq mi)
Population: 560

Languages: Italian, Latin
Religion: Roman Catholic
Currency: Euro
Industries: None.

The Vatican City is the world's smallest state. As the Roman Catholic Church's headquarters, it concerns itself not only with spiritual affairs, but with secular matters. Gold and silver are the colours of the keys to the Kingdom of Heaven, entrusted by Christ to St Peter. The flag is divided vertically into equal bands of yellow (gold) at the hoist and white (silver) at the fly. Within the white section is St Peter's emblem – crossed keys bound with a red cord, set below a papal tiara. The flag was adopted in 1825 and used until 1870, when the Papal States were merged into a unified Italy. Independent status was recognized in 1929 by the Lateran Treaty, which recognizes the Pope's sovereignty.

MALTA
Republic of Malta

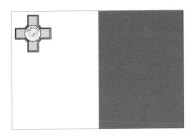

Flag proportions: 2:3
Adopted: 21 September 1964
Capital: Valletta
Area: 316km² (122sq mi)
Population: 405,000
Languages: Maltese, English

Religion: Roman Catholic
Currency: Euro
Exports: Machinery, transport equipment, manufactured goods, chemicals.

Red and white are the colours of the Knights of St John of Jerusalem, who made the island their headquarters after the loss of the island of Rhodes to Islam in 1530. Their emblem, a Maltese cross, appears on the flag and coat of arms of the Grand Master of the order.

Malta was annexed by Britain in 1814, and became a strategic naval base in World War II. As a result, the George Cross, the highest British award for gallantry other than in battle, was awarded to the islanders in 1942 for courage in the face of sustained attack. The George Cross is depicted on the flag in two shades of grey, edged with red, and placed in the chief canton of a flag divided vertically into equal parts of white and red.

SLOVENIA
Republic of Slovenia

Flag proportions: 1:2
Adopted: 24 June 1991
Capital: Ljubljana
Area: 20,273km² (7,827sq mi)
Population: 2,010,000
Language: Slovene

Religion: Roman Catholic
Currency: Euro
Exports: Machinery, transport equipment, basic manufactured goods, chemicals, foodstuffs.

In 1848, a revolt against Austrian domination saw the raising, in the town of Ljubljana, of a tricolour flag with horizontal bands of white over blue over red. The revolt failed and, with the collapse of the Austro-Hungarian Empire in 1918, Slovenia became part of Yugoslavia. In 1946, as a communist republic within Yugoslavia, Slovenia acquired its own flag – a revival of the 1848 tricolour with a gold-bordered red star in the centre.

The present flag, bearing the national arms, was adopted at independence in 1991. The arms depict three white mountain peaks on a blue field, with two wavy blue lines, depicting the coastline, at the base. Above the central peak are three gold stars derived from the ancient arms of the former Duchy of Celje.

CROATIA

Republic of Croatia

Flag proportions: 1:2
Adopted: 22 December 1990
Capital: Zagreb
Area: 56,542km² (20,831sq mi)
Population: 4,442,000
Language: Croat, Serbian

Religion: Roman Catholic
Currency: Kuna
Exports: Transport equipment,
textiles, chemicals, fuels,
foodstuffs.

Croatia was part of Hungary and, later, of Yugoslavia before becoming a semi-independent Marxist state at the end of World War II. During the war, the horizontal tricolour of red over white over blue was used, with the arms of Croatia at the centre. The communist leadership, however, decreed that a gold-edged red star should replace the arms, which were reinstated only when the country gained independence in 1991.

The arms consist of a shield of red and white squares, in a pattern known in heraldry as checky. Above the shield is an arc-shaped crown composed of five inverted shields, each bearing the arms of one of the Croatian regions.

BOSNIA AND HERZEGOVINA

Republic of Bosnia and Herzegovina

Flag proportions: 1:2
Adopted: February 1998
Capital: Sarajevo
Area: 51,129km² (19,741sq mi)
Population: 3,875,000
Language: Serbo-Croat (Serbian)

and Croato-Serb (Croat)
Religion: Sunni Islam, Serbian
Orthodox, Roman Catholic
Currency: Marka
Exports: Metals and other
minerals, cloth, timber, food.

Bosnia and Herzegovina was ruled by the Ottoman Empire from 1463 to 1878, when it was seized by Austria. It formed part of Yugoslavia from 1945 until it broke away in 1992, precipitating a civil war between Muslims, Serbs and Croats which ended with a 1995 peace agreement.

The current flag's yellow triangle represents the shape of the country. Triangles symbolize liberty, equality and fraternity. Blue and yellow recall the flag of the European Union; there is no symbolism associated with the stars. The Republic of Srpska, and the Bosnia and Herzegovina Federation, have their own flags.

SERBIA
Republic of Serbia

Flag proportions: 1:2
Adopted: August 2004
Capital: Belgrade
Area: 77,474km² (25,913sq mi)
Population: 7,441,000
Language: Serbian

Religion: Serbian Orthodox
Currency: Serbian Dinar
Exports: Basic manufactured goods, foodstuffs, raw materials, machinery, transport equipment.

The kingdom of Serbia emerged from Ottoman (Turkish) rule in the nineteenth century, its independence being internationally recognized in 1878. In 1918, Serbia formed the nucleus of the new Kingdom of the Serbs, Croats and Slovenes, which changed its name to Yugoslavia in 1929. In 1945, the country became a federation of six republics, each of which, with the exception of Serbia and Montenegro, seceded in the early 1990s. Serbia and Montenegro formed a confederation in 2003, but Montenegro seceded in 2006. The flag adopted by Serbia in 2004 is virtually the same as that flown in Serbia before 1918, with the addition of the arms of the Obrenovic dynasty (which provided Serbia with kings from 1882 to 1903).

KOSOVO
Kosovo

Flag proportions: 1:2
Adopted: February 2008
Capital: Pristina
Area: 10,887km² (4,203sq mi)
Population: 1,950,000
Language: Albanian

Religion: Sunni Islam
Currency: Euro
Exports: Basic manufactured goods, foodstuffs, raw materials, machinery and transport equipment.

Kosovo was under Ottoman rule until 1912, when Serbia reacquired it after the First Balkan War. It remained part of Serbia, gaining autonomy within Yugoslavia in 1945. Yugoslavia broke up in the early 1990s, and Kosovar nationalism increased when the Serb government carried out repressive measures against Kosovar Albanians. The international community intervened and placed Kosovo under United Nations control in 1999. Kosovo unilaterally declared independence in February 2008, and was recognized by more than 40 (mainly Western) nations. The Kosovar flag depicts an outline of Kosovo with six stars, representing the different ethnic communities in the state.

MONTENEGRO

Montenengro	**Flag proportions:** 2:5	**Religion:** Serbian Orthodox,
	Adopted: July 2004	Montenegrin Orthodox
	Capital: Podgorica	**Currency:** Euro
	Area: 13,812km² (5,333sq mi)	**Exports:** Steel, aluminium, basic
	Population: 620,000	manufactured goods, electricity.
	Language: Serbian	

Montenegro was ruled by the Ottomans (Turks) until independence was recognized in 1878, and in 1910 the state became a kingdom under the native Petrovic dynasty, which had ruled Montenegro as princes. Liberated from Austrian rule in 1918, Montenegro was effectively annexed to the new Serb-dominated state that became Yugoslavia. When Yugoslavia broke up the early 1990s, Montenegro did not secede. However, the loose confederation of Serbia and Montenegro broke up in 2006. Prior to Independence, Montenegro readopted the flag it had flown as a kingdom before 1918, including the arms of the Petrovic dynasty.

MACEDONIA

The Former Yugoslav Republic of Macedonia

Flag proportions: 1:2
Adopted: 6 October 1995
Capital: Skopje
Area: 25,713km² (9,928sq mi)
Population: 2,023,000
Language: Macedonian, Albanian
Religion: Macedonian Orthodox,
Sunni Islam
Currency: Denar
Exports: Foodstuffs, beverages, tobacco, basic manufactured goods, iron and steel, machinery and transport equipment.

After centuries of Turkish rule, Macedonia was briefly part of Serbia (1913–19) before being incorporated into Yugoslavia. The Macedonian flag was the only Yugoslavian provincial flag under the communist regime (1945–91) that did not use Pan-Slavic colours, showing instead a gold-edged red star in the chief canton, on a red field. A controversial new flag, devised before independence in 1992, was abandoned after three years. The present flag displays a gold radiant sun on a red field, with eight rays, both diagonal and parallel to the edges of the flag, and broader at the ends than at the centre. Red and yellow come from the traditional Macedonian coat of arms, a golden lion on a red shield.

ALBANIA
The Republic of Albania

Flag proportions: 5:7
Adopted: 7 April 1992
Capital: Tirana (Tiranë)
Area: 28,748km² (11,100sq mi)
Population: 3,069,000
Language: Albanian (Gheg and Tosk dialects)

Religion: Sunni Islam
Currency: Lek
Exports: Textiles and footwear, asphalt, metals and metallic ores (chromium and copper), foodstuffs, tobacco.

Myth says Albanians are descended from a black eagle. When Albania became an independent kingdom in 1912 after centuries of Turkish rule, the flag featured a double-headed eagle displayed in black on a red field. Albania backed Stalin after World War II, and a gold-edged star was placed above the eagle to symbolize the communist regime. The star was removed after the downfall of communism in Albania in 1992.

The Albanian arms also feature the black double-headed eagle on a red shield. An early version included a gold warrior's helmet, recalling Iskander Bey, an Albanian hero who led an uprising against the Turks in 1443.

GREECE
The Hellenic Republic

Flag proportions: 2:3
Adopted: 22 December 1978
Capital: Athens (Athínai)
Area: 131,957km² (50,949sq mi)
Population: 11,125,000
Language: Greek

Religion: Greek Orthodox
Currency: Euro
Exports: Food and beverages, manufactured goods, petroleum products, chemicals, minerals, textiles, cotton.

Greece, part of the Ottoman Empire from the 14th century until 1829, recalls the struggle for independence from the Turks in its flag. The horizontal stripes (five blue, four white) echo the syllables of the patriots' motto, 'Freedom or Death'; blue represents sea and sky, and white the justness of the Greek cause. Christianity is represented by a white cross in the chief canton. Periodic unrest after World War II saw the king ousted by an army coup in 1967, and the establishment of a democratic republic in 1973. Over the years, the shade of blue in the flag has been altered a few times to express changes in the country's political regime.

CYPRUS

The Republic of Cyprus

Flag proportions: 3:5
Adopted: 16 August 1960
Capital: Nicosia
Area: 9,251km² (3,572sq mi), of which 3,355km² (1,295sq mi) are in the Turkish-controlled zone
Population: 1,023,00 (including

Turkish 'settlers' in the north)
Languages: Greek, Turkish
Religion: Greek Orthodox, Sunni Islam
Currency: Euro, Turkish Lira (in the Turkish Cypriot area)
Exports: Potatoes, citrus fruit.

Its strategic position in the Mediterranean means that Cyprus has a history of invasion and conquest. Part of the Byzantine Empire from AD395, it was taken by England during the Third Crusade (1191) and annexed by the Ottoman Empire in 1571. It fell under British rule in 1878 and became a crown colony in 1925. Since the 1960s, possession of Cyprus has been disputed between Greece and Turkey. In 1974 it was partitioned into a Greek Cypriot area and the Turkish Republic of Northern Cyprus.

The island's map is depicted on its flag in dark yellow (for copper). The white field symbolizes peace and hope, with crossed olive branches for conciliation. The flag is usually flown with the Greek national flag.

TURKEY

The Republic of Turkey

Flag proportions: 15:22
Adopted: 5 June 1936
Capital: Ankara
Area: 779,452km² (300,947sq mi)
Population: 73,875,000

Language: Turkish, Kurdish
Religion: Sunni Islam, Shia Islam
Currency: Turkish lira
Exports: Clothing and textiles, foodstuffs, iron and steel, transportation equipment.

Red has been the dominant colour in Turkish flags since the founding of the Ottoman Empire which, at its height in the 16th century, stretched from North Africa through the Levant to Hungary and Russia's southern borders.

When the white star and crescent appeared on the red flag of the Ottoman Empire in 1793, it was already an established symbol of Islam. The star initially had eight points, but a five-pointed version was used from the mid-19th century. The star is tilted so that one point touches an imaginary line joining the horns of the crescent. Full specifications for this, and all other flags used in Turkey, were drawn up in 1936.

BULGARIA
Republic of Bulgaria

Flag proportions: 3:5
Adopted: 27 November 1990
Capital: Sofia (Sofiya)
Area: 110,993km² (42,855sq mi)
Population: 7,679,000
Language: Bulgarian, Turkish

Religion: Bulgarian Orthodox, Sunni Islam
Currency: Lev
Exports: Clothing, footwear, iron and steel, machinery, food, beverages, tobacco, fuels.

As part of the Ottoman Empire for almost 500 years, Bulgaria had no national flag. On becoming a principality in 1878, it adopted a horizontal tricolour of white over green over red, retaining this when Bulgaria became an independent kingdom in 1908. After the monarchy was abolished in 1946 and a people's republic proclaimed, a coat of arms was added to the white band. The arms were removed in 1990, after the fall of communism, and the flag reverted to the original tricolour. White represents peace, green stands for freedom and the emerging nation, and red the bravery of the people.

ROMANIA
Republic of Romania

Flag proportions: 2:3
Adopted: 27 December 1989
Capital: Bucharest (Bucuresti)
Area: 237,500km² (91,699sq mi)
Population: 21,623,000
Language: Romanian, Hungarian
Religion: Romanian Orthodox

Currency: Leu
Exports: Textiles and shoes, metals and metal products, machinery and transport equipment, minerals, fuels, chemicals, foodstuffs.

The principalities of Wallachia and Moldavia broke from the Ottoman Empire in 1859, uniting as an independent kingdom under a blue-yellow-red vertical tricolour, still the national flag of Romania. Blue came from the Moldavian flag, yellow from Wallachia. Red, common to both, symbolizes Romanian unity. In 1867, the Royal Arms was added to the yellow band, where it remained (with several changes) until replaced with a communist emblem in 1948. After the fall of the Ceausescu regime in 1989, the former coat of arms was restored, with changes, but this no longer appears on the flag.

HUNGARY

Republic of Hungary

Flag proportions: 2:3
Adopted: 1 October 1957
Capital: Budapest
Area: 93,030km² (35,919sq mi)
Population: 10,077,000
Language: Hungarian

Religion: Roman Catholic,
Calvinist Reformed
Currency: Forint
Exports: Machinery and transport
equipment, industrial goods,
consumer goods, foodstuffs.

The kingdom of Hungary was under Austrian control until 1848. When revolution broke out, Hungarian patriots hoisted a red-white-green tricolour, often with a central coat of arms. The colours were probably derived from the historical arms of Hungary, and the stripes inspired by the flag of revolutionary France. Red symbolizes strength, white stands for faithfulness, and green, hope. When Hungary became independent in 1918, the Hungarian arms were added, only to be replaced with appropriate Soviet emblems during the communist era (1949–90). Although restored with democracy in 1990, they no longer appear on the flag.

SLOVAKIA

Slovak Republic

Flag proportions: 2:3
Adopted: 1 September 1993
Capital: Bratislava
Area: 49,035km² (18,933sq mi)
Population: 5,389,000
Language: Slovak, Hungarian
Religion: Roman Catholic,

non-religious
Currency: Slovak Koruna
Exports: Vehicles, machinery,
transport equipment, semi-
manufactured goods, fuels,
chemicals, manufactured goods,
foodstuffs..

Slovakia was under the dual monarchy of Austria-Hungary until 1918, when it became part of Czechoslovakia under the flag now used by the Czech Republic. When Slovakia was an Axis country (1939–45), the horizontal tricolour of white over blue over red was adopted. With the dissolution of Czechoslovakia in 1993, the Slovak arms were added off-centre on the flag to distinguish it from that of Russia.

The arms consist of a stylized blue image of mountains, from which a white patriarchal cross rises against a red field.

MOLDOVA

Republic of Moldova

Flag proportions: 1:2
Adopted: 1990
Capital: Chisinau
Area: 33,873km² (13,078sq mi)
Population: 3,940,000
Language: Romanian (Moldovan)
Religion: Non-religious majority, Romanian (Moldovan) Orthodox minority
Currency: Moldovan Leu
Exports: Food and agricultural goods (fruit and wine), textiles, machinery.

In 1940, parts of the historic principality of Moldavia were partitioned from Romania; the eastern portion becoming the Soviet republic of Moldova and the western part remaining with Romania. It has been independent since 1991.

The flag's colours are similar to those of Romania, but it is distinguished by the Moldovan arms in the central panel. The arms, based on those of the former principality of Moldavia, comprise a red and blue shield and an eagle. The most prominent feature is the head of a bison, an old Moldavian symbol of power and independence. The eagle clasps an olive branch, representing peace, and a mace, representing willingness to defend.

UKRAINE

Ukraine

Flag proportions: 2:3
Adopted: 28 January 1992
Capital: Kiev (Kyiv)
Area: 603,700km² (231,100sq mi)
Population: 6,560,000
Language: Ukrainian, Russian
Religion: Non-religious, Ukrainian Orthodox, Russian Orthodox
Currency: Hryvnia
Exports: Ferrous metals, fuels, machinery and transport equipment, minerals, chemicals, foodstuffs.

Formerly part of Imperial Russia, Ukraine became an independent state in 1918 after the fall of the monarchy and the collapse of a short-lived Russian treaty with Germany. However, within a year, the country was under Soviet control, which lasted until 1991. The flag was banned during the Soviet era, but had been permitted by the Nazis when they occupied Ukraine during World War II. After the war, it was banned again, reappearing as the national flag in 1991, when full independence was gained. The flag is said to resemble the Ukrainian landscape of golden wheat fields stretching to the horizon to meet the blue sky.

BELARUS

Republic of Belarus

Flag proportions: 1:2
Adopted: 7 June 1995
Capital: Minsk
Area: 207,546km²
(80,134sq mi)
Population: 9,751,000
Language: Belarusian

Religion: Non-religious,
Belarusian Orthodox, Roman
Catholic
Currency: Belarusian rouble
Exports: Machinery and
equipment, mineral products,
chemicals, metals, textiles.

The patterned red-and-white vertical stripe along the hoist is derived from a woven pattern that appears on Belarusian national costume. The flag is horizontally divided into thirds, with two thirds red above one third green. Red recalls both sacrifice and victory under a red banner, first in medieval times at Grunwald and then against Fascist invaders in the 1940s. Green signifies spring and revival, and so is the colour of hope. When Belarus gained independence in 1991, the flag chosen was a red-white-red tribar, which was first used in 1918. The present flag, which is similar to that of the former Soviet Byelorussia, was adopted in 1995. The national flag is usually flown from a staff painted golden ochre.

RUSSIA

Russian Federation

Flag proportions: 2:3
Adopted: 11 December 1993
Capital: Moscow (Moskva)
Area: 17,075,400km²
(6,592,810sq mi)
Population: 142,754,000
Language: Russian, Tatar,
Ukrainian
Religion: Non-religious,

Russian Orthodox, Sunni Islam
Currency: Rouble
Exports: Fuels and lubricants
(including petroleum and petroleum
products and natural gas), timber
and forestry products, ferrous and
non-ferrous metals, chemicals,
precious metals, machinery and
transport equipment.

Tsar Peter the Great visited the Netherlands in 1697 and, impressed by the Dutch tricolour, adopted it for the Russian merchant fleet, altering the order of the stripes to white, blue and red. This became the national flag in the 19th century but, after the Bolshevik revolution of 1917, the Red Flag with its hammer, sickle and star was adopted. The tricolour reappeared in 1990 as communism faltered. Following the collapse of the Soviet Union in 1991, it emerged as the flag of the new state.

GEORGIA

Republic of Georgia

Flag proportions: 2:3
Adopted: 14 January 2004
Capital: Tbilisi
Area: 69,492km² (26,831sq mi), including Abkhazia and South Ossetia
Population: 701,000 (including an estimated 300,000 in Abkhazia and South Ossetia)

Language: Georgian, Russian, Armenian
Religion: Non-religious, Georgian Orthodox, Sunni Islam
Currency: Lari
Exports: Scrap metals, machinery, chemicals, fuel re-exports, food products (particularly citrus fruit, tea and wine).

The kingdoms composing Georgia were part of the Russian empire throughout the 19th century. However, Georgia enjoyed a brief period of independence from 1918–21, during which its national flag was dark red with a canton of black over white horizontal stripes. That flag was revived in 1991 after the collapse of the USSR, when Georgia again became independent. In 2003, a revolution led by the National Movement against the government resulted in the adoption of its banner as the new national flag. This 'flag of five crosses' emphasizes the Georgian Orthodox faith.

ARMENIA

The Republic of Armenia

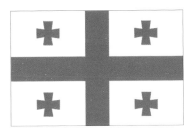

Flag proportions: 1:2
Adopted: 24 August 1990
Capital: Yerevan
Area: 29,743km² (11,484sq mi)
Population: 3,219,000
Language: Armenian
Religion: Armenian Apostolic

(Orthodox)
Currency: Dram
Exports: Jewellery (particularly diamonds), scrap metals, various machinery and transport equipment, minerals (mainly copper), electricity.

For several centuries Armenia was part of the Ottoman Empire. Following World War I it was briefly independent, before becoming a Soviet republic in 1922. During the Soviet era, the horizontal tricolour of red above blue above orange was banned, but it was raised again as the national flag of the republic of Armenia in 1991. Red represents the sun's energy, along with the blood spilt during the struggle for independence; blue is for hope and clear skies, and orange is for the blessing of crops at harvest.

AZERBAIJAN

The Republic of Azerbaijan

Caspian
Sea

Georgia AZERBAIJAN

Black
Sea

Armenia

Iran

Flag proportions: 1:2
Adopted: 5 February 1991
Capital: Baku (Bakí)
Area: 86,600km² (33,400sq mi)
Population: 8,427,000, including
Karabkah

Language: Azeri
Religion: Shia Islam, Sunni Islam
Currency: Manat
Exports: Petroleum and petroleum
products, natural gas, machinery,
cotton, food products.

Azerbaijan's brief spell of independence, following the 1918 collapse of the Ottoman Empire, ended with annexation by Soviet Russia in 1920. The flag created to celebrate independence was prohibited by the new rulers, and was only raised again in 1991 as the national flag. The flag is a horizontal tricolour of blue above red above green: blue is the representative colour, green is for Islam and red represents energy and progress. At the centre of the flag, within the red band, are a white crescent and an eight-pointed star, the emblems of Islam. Each point of the star represents one group of the Turkic peoples.

WESTERN AND
SOUTHERN ASIA

Asia is the largest and highest continent. At its western end, abutting Europe, is the Middle East. Here is land held sacred by many faiths, where areas of rich heritage are juxtaposed with modern settlements that are bitterly contested. Here, too, ancient civilizations have left abundant evidence in the 'fertile crescent' along the rivers Tigris and Euphrates.

In the Middle East and Gulf States, wealth is measured in colossal oil reserves. Shared religions, history and ethnicity have not been protection against war, however, as demonstrated by the long struggle between Iraq and Iran, Iraq's invasion of Kuwait, and the involvement of western powers in military conflict in the region.

Further afield, the partition of India that followed the withdrawal of British imperial power in 1947 was based on religion, and resulted in the creation of Pakistan. This primarily Muslim country consisted of two separate territories, which led to the 1971 political separation of East Pakistan (now Bangladesh), situated around the Ganges delta.

Afghanistan once shared a frontier with British India, but the Khyber Pass now crosses into Pakistan. The northern Afghan border was a source of tension for more than a century, ending with Russian invasion and, subsequently, an armed American presence.

The southern portion of the area being covered extends from Pakistan in the west, through India, Nepal and Bhutan to Bangladesh, and protrudes some 3000km (1864mi) into the Indian Ocean as far as Sri Lanka. Here are some of the most densely populated places in the world, where 18 principal languages are heard, in addition to many regional dialects.

AT A GLANCE

Largest country: India
Smallest country: Maldives
Largest city: Mumbai (Bombay), India
Major cities: Almaty, Amman, Baghdad, Beirut, Calcutta, Chennai (Madras), Damascus, Delhi, Dhaka, Kabul, Karachi, Kolkata (Calcutta), Lahore, Riyadh, Tehran.
Highest point: Mt Everest, Nepal and China – 8,850m (29,035ft).

Lowest point: Dead Sea, Israel/Jordan – 392m (1,286ft) below sea level.
Longest rivers: Euphrates, Syria/Iraq – 2,800km (1,740mi); Indus, India – 2,880km (1,790mi); Ganges, India – 2,510km (1,553mi).
Largest lake: Aral Sea, Kazakhstan and Uzbekistan – 17,160km² (6,625sq mi).

Western and Southern Asia

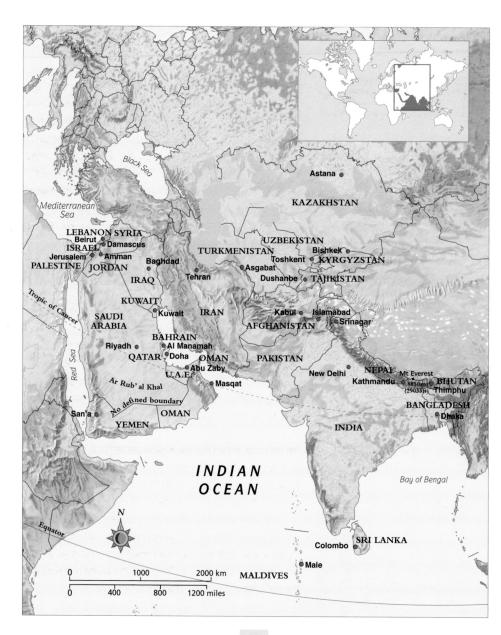

Black Sea

Mediterranean
Sea

Astana

KAZAKHSTAN

LEBANON SYRIA
Beirut ● Damascus
ISRAEL
Jerusalem ● Amman
PALESTINE / JORDAN
Baghdad
IRAQ
Tehran

UZBEKISTAN
TURKMENISTAN   Bishkek ●
Toshkent ● KYRGYZSTAN
Asgabat
Dushanbe ● TAJIKISTAN

Tropic of Cancer

KUWAIT
SAUDI   Kuwait   IRAN
ARABIA
BAHRAIN
Riyadh ●   ● Al Manamah
QATAR ● Doha OMAN   PAKISTAN
● Abu Zaby
U.A.E
Ar Rub' al Khal   ● Masqat

Kabul ● Islamabad
AFGHANISTAN   ● Srinagar

New Delhi   NEPAL Mt Everest
Kathmandu ● 8850m BHUTAN
(29035ft) Thimphu

No defined boundary

BANGLADESH
● Dhaka

San'a ●
YEMEN
OMAN

INDIA

Red Sea

INDIAN
OCEAN

Bay of Bengal

N

Equator

SRI LANKA
Colombo ●

● Male

0   1000   2000 km   MALDIVES
0   400   800   1200 miles

SYRIA

The Arab Republic of Syria

Flag proportions: 2:3
Adopted: 3 April 1980
Capital: Damascus (Dimashq)
Area: 185,180km²
(71,498sq mi), including the
disputed Golan Heights
Population: 18,356,000

Language: Arabic, Kurdish
Religion: Sunni Islam, Shia Islam
Currency: Syrian pound
Exports: Crude petroleum and
petroleum products, fruit and
vegetables, textiles and fabrics,
meat.

Four hundred years of Turkish domination ended in 1920 when Syria became a French mandate. The French created two flags for Syria, which were replaced by a tricolour of green above white above black with three red stars in the centre, under which the country achieved independence in 1946. Each star represented a province. When Syria and Egypt formed the United Arab Republic (UAR) in 1958 the colours were changed to red, white and black, with two stars. After briefly reverting to the earlier flag, Syria adopted the UAR flag with three stars and a gold central coat of arms, which was then abandoned when the current flag was adopted.

LEBANON

The Republic of Lebanon

Flag proportions: 2:3
Adopted: 7 December 1943
Capital: Beirut (Bayrût)
Area: 10,201km² (3,939sq mi)
Population: 3,754,000
Language: Arabic
Religion: Shia Islam, Sunni Islam,

Maronite (Uniat Roman Cathollic),
Druze
Currency: Lebanese pound
Exports: Precious stones and
jewellery, chemicals, consumer
goods, foodstuffs, tobacco,
construction materials, textiles.

The red bands in the Lebanese tricolour are each half the depth of the white band on which a cedar tree is represented in green. When Lebanon was mandated to France after World War I, the *Tricolore* was flown with a depiction of the cedar at the centre. Officially, the colours of the current flag are red, white and green and the cedar is not intended to be depicted 'proper' (lifelike, with brownish trunk and branches).

Cedars and Lebanon have been linked since the time of King Solomon, in the 10th century BC. The cedar is the symbol of the country's Maronite Christian community, and depicts immortality.

JORDAN

The Hashemite Kingdom of Jordan

Flag proportions: 1:2
Adopted: 16 April 1928
Capital: Amman
Area: 89,342km² (34,492sq mi)
Population: 5,103,000
Language: Arabic

Religion: Sunni Islam
Currency: Jordanian dinar
Exports: Clothing, phosphates, fertilizers, potash, fruit and vegetables, nuts, manufactured goods, pharmaceuticals.

The Pan-Arab colours first flew in 1917 to rally forces to the Arab Revolt against Turkish rule. Jordan was mandated to Britain, but achieved a measure of independence in 1928 when the present flag was raised. The black, white and green bands represent the Arab Abbasid, Umayyad and Fatimid dynasties respectively. The red isosceles triangle at the hoist represents the Hashemite dynasty, whose descendants are the rulers of Jordan. The seven-pointed star at the centre of the triangle depicts the unity of the Arab peoples in Jordan, as well as the seven verses that open the Koran and provide the basis for Islamic belief.

ISRAEL

The State of Israel

Flag proportions: 8:11
Adopted: 12 November 1948
Capital: Jerusalem (Yerushalayim)
Area: 21,946km² (8473sq mi)
(including the disputed East Jerusalem and Golan Heights)
Population: 6,991,000
(including the disputed East

Jerusalem and Golan Heights)
Languages: Hebrew, Arabic
Religion: Judaism, Sunni Islam
Currency: New sheqel
Exports: Machinery and transport equipment, software, cut diamonds, chemicals, clothing and textiles, food and beverages.

The design of the flag predates the State of Israel by more than 50 years, although the Shield of David was used for centuries as a symbol of Judaism. The outline of the six-pointed star is also known as the Seal of Solomon. The flag's blue and white colours represent the Hebrew prayer shawl. As a Jewish symbol, the star was first used on a flag in the 14th century by the Jewish community of Prague. Flagpoles from which the Israeli flag is flown sometimes have their lower third painted blue, with the remainder painted white.

SAUDI ARABIA

Kingdom of Saudi Arabia

Flag proportions: 2:3
Adopted: 15 March 1973
Capital: Riyadh (Al Riyad)
Area: 2,149,690km²
(830,003sq mi)
Population: 22,678,000

Language: Arabic
Religion: Sunni Islam
Currency: Riyal
Exports: Petroleum,
petrochemicals.

Green, the colour of Islam, is believed to have been the favourite colour of the Prophet Mohammed. On both sides of the Saudi flag, the Muslim statement of faith, 'There is no God but Allah, Mohammed is the Prophet of Allah', appears in white Arabic letters, from the viewer's right to left. Below the inscription, a straight-bladed, single-edged sword represents justice. It depicts the sword of King Ibn Saud, who founded the kingdom in 1932 by uniting the kingdoms of Hejaz and Nejd. An absolute monarchy with no written constitution, Saudi Arabia is ruled in accordance with Islamic law, and derives immense wealth from its oil reserves.

YEMEN

Republic of Yemen

Flag proportions: 2:3
Adopted: 22 May 1990
Capital: Sana'a
Area: 527,970km²
(203,850sq mi)
Population: 19,722,000

Language: Arabic
Religion: Sunni Islam, Shia Zaydi
Islam
Currency: Yemeni Rial
Exports: Petroleum, coffee,
dried fish.

North Yemen was part of the Ottoman Empire, while South Yemen was under British colonial rule until 1967. The radical politics of the south and the conservative politics of the north prevented unification. Even after a revolution in North Yemen, each republic maintained its own statehood and flag. South Yemen flew a red-white-black tricolour, with a blue triangle at the hoist and a red star for socialism. North Yemen also flew a red-white-black tricolour, but with a green five-pointed star at the centre. The unified flag, with the Pan-Arab colours, represents the tricolour that had been basic to both territories.

OMAN

Sultanate of Oman

Flag proportions: 1:2
Adopted: 18 November 1995
Capital: Muscat (Masqat)
Area: 309,500km²
(119,500sq mi)
Population: 2,508,000

Language: Arabic, Baluchi
Religion: Ibadiyah Islam, Sunni
Islam, Shia Islam
Currency: Omani Rial
Exports: Petroleum, re-exports,
fish, metals, textiles.

Oman's capital, Muscat, has been a trading post for centuries. Given its strategic location, it is not surprising that the country changed rulers many times. Red has long been the dominant colour in the region. The Omani flag may be seen either as bands of white and green on a red field, or as a horizontal tricolour with a broad red band at the hoist. White is associated with a former imam of Oman, and depicts peace. Green relates to the Sultanate's Jebel Akhdar highlands, and is the colour of Islam and of fertility. At the hoist is the emblem of the ruling dynasty: crossed swords and a gold traditional dagger.

UNITED ARAB EMIRATES

United Arab Emirates

Flag proportions: 1:2
Adopted: 2 December 1971
Capital: Abu Dhabi (Abu Zaby)
Area: 83,600km² (32,280sq mi)
Population: 3,769,000
Language: Arabic, languages of
the Indian subcontinent

Religion: Sunni Islam, Shia Islam,
Hindu
Currency: Dirham
Exports: Crude and refined
petroleum, natural gas, re-exports,
dried fish, dates.

The United Arab Emirates (UAE), a federation of the emirates of Abu Dhabi, Ajman, Dubai, Fujairah, Sharjah, Umm al Qaiwain and Ras al Khaimah, was formed in 1971 from the Trucial States (a name given by the British for administrative purposes when the area came under a treaty in 1853). The seven hereditary *emirs* (sheiks) serve on the federal Supreme Council of Rulers of the UAE. Abu Dhabi is the capital and Dubai the chief port.

Pan-Arab colours were adopted for the united flag: green for fertility, white for neutrality, black for the reserves of oil, and red for the original emirates' flags.

BAHRAIN

The Kingdom of Bahrain

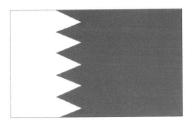

Flag proportions: 3:5
Adopted: 16 February 2002
Capital: Manama (Al-Manamah)
Area: 716km² (277sq mi)
Population: 651,000
Language: Arabic, languages of the Indian subcontinent

Religion: Shia Islam, Sunni Islam
Currency: Bahrain Dinar
Exports: Petroleum, aluminium, textiles, basic manufactured goods.

Bahrain comprises a group of islands in the Gulf, linked by a causeway to Saudi Arabia. The unusual junction of colours in the flag has its origins in a treaty of 1820, whereby friendly states in the Persian Gulf undertook to border their flags with white so that they would not be mistaken for pirate flags. Originally the line was straight but it was serrated in 1932 to distinguish the flag of Bahrain from those of its neighbouring territories. The flag's five indentations stand for the five basic requirements of Islam. No fewer than nine legal articles describe and govern the use of the Bahraini flag.

QATAR

State of Qatar

Flag proportions: 11:28
Adopted: 1949
Capital: Doha (Ad Dawhah)
Area: 11,427km² (4,412sq mi)
Population: 838,000
Language: Arabic, languages of the Indian subcontinent, Iranian (Farsi)

Religion: Sunni Isla, Shia Islam
Currency: Qatari Riyal
Exports: Petroleum, fertilizers, steel, chemicals.

The Al-Khalifa clan ruled both Qatar and Bahrain in the 18th and early 19th centuries under a plain red flag. A revolt in 1868 led to the independence of Qatar, and four years later the Ottoman Turks established a protectorate in the area. After World War I the British replaced the Ottomans, and it was around this time that the national flag was established. There were many variations in the flag's design, however, and a standard pattern was not finalized until 1949. The finalized design recalled the flag of Bahrain, with which Qatar was long associated. The flag has remained unchanged ever since, even when Qatar became independent in 1971.

KUWAIT

State of Kuwait

Flag proportions: 1:2
Adopted: 24 November 1961
Capital: Kuwait City (Al Kuwayt)
Area: 17,818km² (6,880sq mi)
Population: 2,213,000
Language: Arabic, languages of the Indian subcontinent
Religion: Sunni Islam, Shia Islam
Currency: Kuwaiti Dinar
Exports: Petroleum and petroleum products, fertilizers.

When Kuwait gained independence in 1961, having been under British rule since 1899, a flag in the Pan-Arab colours was adopted. The tricolour of green above white above red has a black trapezium at the hoist. An official explanation of the Pan-Arab colours states that black symbolizes the defeat of enemies, white is for purity, green is for fertile land and red is for enemies' blood on Kuwaiti swords. An alternative explanation is that white is for honour, black is for the sand raised by Kuwaiti horsemen in their battle for freedom, green is for the fields and red is for gallantry.

IRAQ

Republic of Iraq

Flag proportions: 2:3
Adopted: January 2008
Capital: Baghdad
Area: 434,128km²
(167,618sq mi)
Population: 27,475,000
Language: Arabic, Kurdish
Religion: Shia Islam, Sunni Islam
Currency: Iraqi Dinar
Exports: Crude petroleum and petroleum products.

Iraqi flags have featured the Pan-Arab colours ever since the Arab Revolt of 1917. The basic pattern that is currently in use was devised in anticipation of a closer union with Egypt and Syria. Three five-pointed green stars were placed in a row in the central band of the horizontal tricolour of red above white above black. The union did not take place, but the design remained. The Islamic phrase, *Allahu Akbar* ('God is Great'), in green Arabic script (in the handwriting of Iraqi dictator Saddam Hussein), was added to the central band during the 1991 Gulf War. However, after the fall of Saddam, the three stars were dropped and the script was changed to decorative Kufic script.

IRAN

The Islamic Republic of Iran

Iraq

IRAN

Afghanistan

The Gulf

Pakistan

Flag proportions: 4:7
Adopted: 29 July 1980
Capital: Tehran
Area: 1,641,918km² (633,945sq mi)
Population: 70,473,000
Language: Farsi (Persian),
Azeri, Kurdish
Religion: Shia Islam
Currency: Rial
Exports: Petroleum, natural gas, chemicals, carpets, fruits, pistachios, iron, steel.

After the overthrow of the monarchy in 1979, the new Islamic Republic introduced a tricolour of green above white above red, with a red central device. The colours have been the national colours of Iran since the late 19th century. At the junction of the white band with the green and red are stylized Kufic inscriptions of the phrase *Allahu Akbar* ('God is Great'), repeated 22 times, because victory in the revolution occurred on the 22nd day of the 11th month of the Iranian calendar. The central device is composed of emblems, including crescents and a sword, which together symbolize the five principles of Islam.

AFGHANISTAN

Afghanistan

Turkmenistan   Tajikistan

Iran

AFGHANISTAN

Pakistan

Flag proportions: 1:2
Adopted: June 2002
Capital: Kabul
Area: 645,807km² (249,348sq mi)
Population: 22,576,000
Language: Dari (Persian), Pashto, Uzbek
Religion: Sunni Islam, Shia Islam
Currency: Afghani
Exports: Opium (illegally exported), dried fruit and nuts, carpets and rugs, wools and hides, cotton, precious and semiprecious stones.

Afghanistan's political changes have resulted in almost 20 flags since 1900. Following the ousting of the Taliban in 2001, the transitional government adopted a flag comprising a vertical tricolour of black, red and green. Black recalls flags previously flown in Afghanistan, while green is the colour of Islam. At the centre is the national arms. Enclosed within a wreath of grain is a mosque, showing the *mihrab* (recess in the wall that indicates Mecca's direction) and a *minbar* (pulpit). Above the mosque is written, 'there is no God but Allah, and Mohammed is the Prophet of Allah'. The inscription *Allahu Akbar* also appears.

TURKMENISTAN

The Republic of Turkmenistan

Flag proportions: 2:3
Adopted: 3 March 2000
Capital: Ashgabat
Area: 488,100km²
(186,500sq mi)
Population: 5,673,000
Language: Turkmen,

Uzbek, Russian
Religion: Sunni Islam
Currency: Manat
Exports: Natural gas, petroleum
and petroleum products, cotton,
textiles.

Turkmenistan's flag celebrates its culture. On a green field a white Islamic crescent is placed in the chief canton with the horns pointing to the hoist. Five five-pointed white stars represent new regions defined in the 1992 constitution. At the hoist, a multicoloured vertical band depicts the hand-knotted carpets for which Turkmenistan is renowned. Five *guls* (medallions) represent traditional patterns, with the border *guls* depicting minor patterns. Turkmenistan gained independence in 1991 and declared a policy of neutrality in 1995, which was accepted by the UN. To symbolize this policy, in 1997 two olive branches were placed below the *guls*.

UZBEKISTAN

The Republic of Uzbekistan

Flag proportions: 1:2
Adopted: 18 November 1991
Capital: Tashkent
Area: 447,000km²
(172,700sq mi)
Population: 26,700,000

Language: Uzbek, Russian
Religion: Sunni Islam
Currency: Sum
Exports: Cotton, gold, petroleum,
natural gas, fertilizers, metals,
foodstuffs.

The post-communist flag of Uzbekistan is a tricolour of blue above white above green, with a narrow red stripe at the junction of the colours. In the chief canton, all in the blue band, a white crescent and 12 five-pointed white stars are arranged in rows: three above four above five. The crescent, as a waxing moon, represents the new republic, with a star for each month of the year. Blue is for sky and water, white is for peace and green is for fertility. The red stripes signify the life force of all people. Despite being a predominantly Muslim country, Uzbekistan's crescent is described in terms of growth rather than religion.

KAZAKHSTAN

Republic of Kazakhstan

Flag proportions: 1:2
Adopted: 4 June 1992
Capital: Astana
Area: 2,717,300km²
(1,049,200sq mi)
Population: 15,218,000
Language: Kazakh, Russian

Religion: Sunni Islam, non-religious, Russian Orthodox
Currency: Tenge
Exports: Oil and natural gas, rolled ferrous metals and refined copper, chemicals, machinery, cereals, wool, meat, coal.

'National ornamentation' is the term used to describe the gold embroidery-like pattern at the hoist of Kazakhstan's flag that is reminiscent of features on the flags of Belarus and Turkmenistan. The field is light blue, for the vast skies of the Kazakhstan plains. On the field a *berkut* (steppe eagle), flies horizontally with outstretched wings. Above the eagle, half framed by its wings, is a sun with short rays. Together they depict freedom and the Kazakh people's aspirations.

TAJIKISTAN

Republic of Tajikistan

Flag proportions: 1:2
Adopted: 24 November 1992
Capital: Dushanbe
Area: 143,100km²
(55,300sq mi)
Population: 6,920,000

Language: Tajik, Uzbek
Religion: Sunni Islam, Shia Islam
Currency: Tajik rouble
Exports: Aluminium, electricity, cotton fibre, fruit, vegetable oil, textiles.

Red, white and green are the same colours as the flag of the former Tadzhik Soviet Socialist Republic. Red symbolizes the sun and victory, green represents fruits, and white is the colour of cotton, the country's principal crop. Within the white band is a gold crown below an arc of seven five-pointed stars. The crown denotes the country's sovereign independence, while in Tajik culture the number seven embodies all human virtues. According to legend, heaven has seven orchards separated by seven mountains, each with a star at its summit. Together, the symbols represent friendship between nations and unity of all classes.

KYRGYZSTAN

Republic of Kyrgyzstan

Flag proportions: 3:5
Adopted: 3 March 1992
Capital: Bishkek
Area: 198,500km²
(76,600sq mi)
Population: 5,162,000
Language: Kyrgyz, Russian, Uzbek

Religion: Sunni Islam, non-religious
Currency: Som
Exports: Cotton and wool, food products (particularly meat), metals (gold and mercury), light manufactures, electricity, footwear.

Although it declared independence in 1991, Kyrgyzstan only adopted its flag the following year. 'Kyrgyz' means red, the colour associated with a traditional hero, Manas the Noble, who united the 40 tribes of Kyrgyzstan. In the centre of the red field is a gold sun, a symbol of light and purity. The individual rays represent the tribes, while the lines across the sun depict the framework of a traditional Kyrgyz yurt, the tent in which nomadic peoples celebrate the virtues of home and family, the unity of space and time and the beginning of life itself.

PAKISTAN

The Islamic Republic of Pakistan

Flag proportions: 2:3
Adopted: 14 August 1947
Capital: Islamabad
Area: 796,095km²(307,374sq mi), excluding Pakistani-held areas of Kashmir (Azad Kashmir) and the disputed Northern Areas (Gilgit, Baltistan and Diamir)
Population: 156,483,000

Language: Urdu, Punjabi, Pashto, Sindhi
Religion: Sunni Islam, Shia Islam, Ismaili Islam
Currency: Pakistan rupee
Exports: Textiles, clothing, cotton yarn, rice, leather goods, chemicals, sporting goods, basic manufactured goods, carpets.

Pakistan became an independent Muslim state following the partition of British India in 1947. The green flag with a white star and crescent was designed by Mohammed Ali Jinnah who, as leader of the Muslim League, campaigned for Pakistan's independence and became its first governor general. Green is the colour of Islam, the white crescent signifies progress, and the five-pointed star symbolizes light and knowledge. The white vertical stripe at the hoist was originally said to stand for peace and prosperity.

72

INDIA

Republic of India

Flag proportions: 2:3
Adopted: 15 August 1947
Capital: New Delhi
Area: 3,287,263km² (1,269,219sq mi) including 121,667km² (44,976sq mi) of Jammu and Kashmir claimed by India but occupied by Pakistan and China

Population: 1,027,000,000
Language: Hindi, English, Telegu, Bengali, Marathi, Tamil, Urdu, Gujarati, Kannada, Malayalam
Religion: Hindu, Sunni Islam
Currency: Indian rupee
Exports: Textiles, clothing, diamonds, jewellery, chemicals.

The horizontal tricolour of orange, white and green recalls the flag of the Indian National Congress (now the Congress Party), which was founded in 1885 to seek independence from British colonial rule. Orange stands for Hinduism, courage and sacrifice; white for the hope of peace; and green for faith and chivalry. At independence in 1947, the flag was modified by the addition of a blue wheel at the centre. Blue represents the ocean and sky, while in Buddhism the spinning wheel represents the inevitability of existence. The 24 spokes of the wheel correspond with the hours in a day.

BANGLADESH

People's Republic of Bangladesh

Flag proportions: 3:5
Adopted: 25 January 1972
Capital: Dhaka
Area: 147,570km² (56,977sq mi)
Population: 129,247,000
Language: Bengali

Religion: Sunni Islam, Hindu
Currency: Taka
Exports: Clothing, jute goods, hides and leather, frozen fish, prawns.

Bangladesh was established as the eastern province of Pakistan at the partition of India in 1947. It was substantially different in culture and language from West Pakistan, resulting in decades of resentment. Following a civil war that precipitated a massive refugee crisis, Bangladesh finally gained independence in 1971. On the flag, green is for the land, fertility and Islam. The red disc, set slightly towards the hoist, symbolizes the rising sun of independence after the blood-drenched struggle.

NEPAL

Nepal

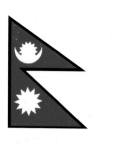

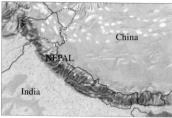

Flag proportions: 4:3
Adopted: 16 December 1962
Capital: Kathmandu
Area: 147,181km² (56,827sq mi)
Population: 23,078,000
Language: Nepali, Maithili,

Bhojpuri
Religion: Hindu, Buddhist
Currency: Nepalese rupee
Exports: Carpets, textiles and
clothing, leather goods, jute,
foodstuffs.

The unique shape of the Nepalese flag is based on two triangular pennants once flown by rival branches of the Rana dynasty. The pennants represent the Himalaya mountains and the country's two religions, Buddhism and Hinduism. As Nepal was until recently a monarchy, the crescent in the upper part depicts the royal house, and the sun in the lower part, the Rana family (which formerly provided the hereditary prime minister). The sun and moon reflect hope, and crimson is the colour of the rhododendron, Nepal's national flower. It also stands for victory in war. The blue border signifies peace. In 2008 the Maoists won parliamentary elections and abolished the monarchy; the flag remains unchanged at the time of publication.

BHUTAN

The Kingdom of Bhutan

Flag proportions: 2:3
Adopted: 1971
Capital: Thimphu
Area: 46,500km² (17,954sq mi)
Population: 672,000
Language: Dzongkha

(Bhutanese),Nepali
Religion: Buddhist, Hindu
Currency: Ngultrum
Exports: Electricity, cardamom,
gypsum, timber, fruit and
vegetables, handicrafts.

Bhutan means 'Land of the Dragon', and the dragon has been associated with the country since about 1200. Thunder was believed to be the sound of dragons roaring, and a religious sect, the Drukpas, claimed the 'thunder dragon' as their emblem, shown in white to symbolize purity and loyalty. Jewels clasped in its claws denote wealth, and the snarling mouth suggests the strength of the deities protecting the country. The field is diagonally divided to represent spiritual and temporal authority in Bhutan. Orange is for the Drukpa monasteries and Buddhist religious practice, while saffron is the colour of the reigning Wangchuk dynasty.

SRI LANKA

The Democratic Socialist Republic of
Sri Lanka

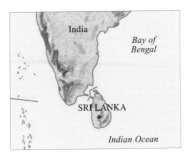

Flag proportions: 1:2
Adopted: 7 September 1978
Capital: Colombo (administrative capital), Kotte (legislative capital)
Area: 65,610km² (25,332sq mi)
Population: 19,886,000
Languages: Sinhala, Tamil

Religion: Buddhist, Hindu,
Sunni Islam
Currency: Sri Lankan rupee
Exports: Textiles and clothing,
tea, gemstones, coconut products,
petroleum products.

The gold lion clasping a sword was the flag of Ceylon prior to 1815, when the island became a British colony. The lion signifies strength and nobility, the sword represents authority, crimson is for national pride and the yellow border symbolizes Buddhism. After independence in 1948, the lion flag was flown again. In 1951, vertical bands of green and saffron were added to represent the Muslim and Hindu Tamil communities. In 1972, when Ceylon became Sri Lanka, four pipul leaves were added. These represent the tree under which Gautama Siddhartha sat when he received enlightenment and became the Buddha, along with the values of love, compassion, empathy and equanimity.

MALDIVES

The Republic of Maldives

Flag proportions: 2:3
Adopted: 26 July 1965
Capital: Malé
Area: 298km² (115sq mi)
Population: 299,000

Language: Dhivehi
Religion: Sunni Islam
Currency: Rufiyaa
Exports: Dried fish, canned fish,
frozen tuna, clothing, dried tuna.

The 'Land of a Thousand Islands' was long a sultanate under British protection. In 1965 it achieved independence and altered its national flag by removing a vertical band at the hoist, made up of black and white diagonal stripes. The green central panel, with or without a white crescent, was added early in the 20th century. Green represents peace and prosperity, as well as palm trees, which are regarded as the islands' life source. Red is for blood shed for independence, and the white crescent is the symbol of Islam.

EASTERN AND SOUTHEAST ASIA

The Far East includes China, Japan, Mongolia, Taiwan and Korea. Population density is erratic, anything from 1.5 people per km² in Mongolia to Macau's 30,000. Climate too is extreme, its principal feature being the monsoon rains, but the same broad region includes the Gobi Desert.

The Philippines are traditionally considered to be the transition point between the Far East and Southeast Asia. The latter region includes many islands and peninsulas, most of which are drained by large rivers, such as the Mekong and Irrawaddy. Southeast Asia comprises Vietnam, Cambodia, Laos, Thailand, Malaysia, Indonesia and Myanmar (formerly Burma).

There are many manufacturing centres, the longest established, on average, being those of Japan which, ironically, has few natural resources. Attempts to secure raw materials were behind militant Japanese expansion before and during World War II. The fighting did not end with Hiroshima, Nagasaki and military withdrawal. Although peace was in sight, the Soviet Union declared war on Japan, thereby laying the foundation for an enduring Communist presence in the north.

Colonial powers, notably France and Britain, came under fire from independence movements, some of them Communist-backed. France withdrew from Indochina (Vietnam, Laos and Cambodia) while the Communist Chinese pushed the Nationalist Chinese from the mainland onto Formosa (now Taiwan). The decade-long war in Vietnam also disrupted the administration in neighbouring countries. In terms of a century-old treaty with China, the last British Union Flag in the region was lowered over Hong Kong in 1997, but the territory's pragmatic administration has seen no loss of revenue.

AT A GLANCE

Largest country: China
Smallest country: Singapore
Largest city: Tokyo, Japan
Major cities: Bangkok, Beijing, Hong Kong, Jakarta, Kuala Lumpur, Manila, Osaka, Shanghai, Tianjin, Tokyo.
Highest point: Mt Everest, China/Nepal 8,850m (29,035ft).

Lowest point: Turpan Basin, China – 154m (505ft) below sea level.
Longest river: Chang Jiang (also called Yangtze), China – 6,300km (3,915mi).
Largest lake: Tônlé Sap, Cambodia – 2,700km² (1,040sq mi); following monsoon 16,000km² (6,180sq mi).

Eastern and Southeast Asia

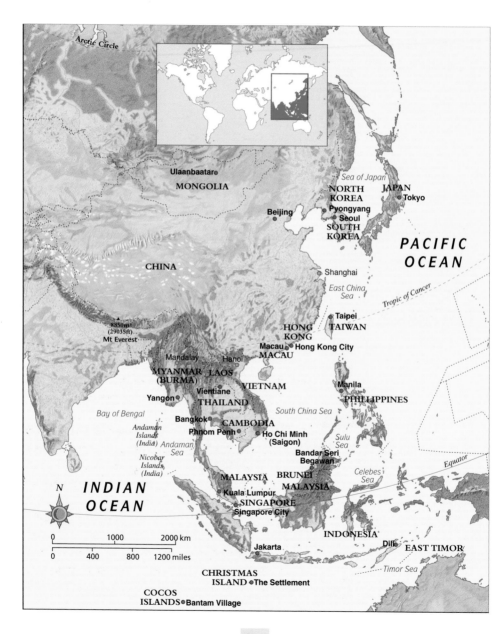

CHINA

The People's Republic of China

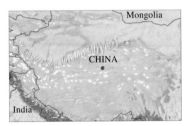

Flag proportions: 2:3
Adopted: 1 October 1949
Capital: Beijing
Area: 9,559,686km²
(3,690,998sq mi) excluding
Taiwan, Hong Kong and Macau
Population: 1,241,053,000
Language: Chinese (Mandarin),
Wu, Cantonese (Yüeh), Xiang,

Min, Hakka
Religion: Chinese folk religions
(including Daoism), non-religious
and atheist, Buddhist
Currency: Yuan
Exports: Machinery, equipment,
textiles, clothing, footwear, toys,
sporting goods, minerals, metal
products, electrical goods.

The Chinese flag was designed to be 'modest and majestic'. Red, the traditional colour of China, also stands for communism. The large yellow star stands for communist ideology, while the four small stars depict the regions of China. Together, the stars echo the importance of the number five in Chinese philosophy. China's first national flag (1872), depicted the blue dragon of the Manchu dynasty on a yellow field. Decades later, clashes between nationalist and communist forces led to several flags being flown prior to the establishment of the People's Republic in 1949.

HONG KONG

Hong Kong Special Administrative Region

Flag proportions: 2:3
Adopted: 1 July 1997
Capital: Hong Kong (Xianggang)
Area: 1,076km² (415sq mi)
Population: 6,708,000
Language: Cantonese, English

Religion: Traditional Chinese folk
religions (including Daoism)
Currency: Hong Kong dollar
Exports: Electrical and electronic
equipment, textiles, clothing,
shoes, watches, toys, plastic.

Formerly part of China, Hong Kong was occupied by Britain in 1841 and ceded by China in 1842. The Kowloon Peninsula was acquired in 1860 and the New Territories were secured under a 99-year lease. As a British crown colony, a Blue Ensign, depicting the local coat of arms, was flown. When the end of the leasehold approached, sovereignty of Hong Kong was transferred to China in 1997 in exchange for an assurance that a capitalist economy would be retained for 50 years. Hong Kong is now a special administrative region of China. Its new flag has a red field and a stylized white flower of the bauhinia tree. The red stars within the five petals are derived from the Chinese flag.

MACAU

Macau Special Administrative Region

Flag proportions: 2:3
Adopted: 20 December 1999
Capital: Macau (Aomén)
Area: 27.5km² (10.5sq mi)
Population: 502,000
Languages: Cantonese, Portuguese
Religion: Buddhist, Roman

Catholic, traditional Chinese
folk religions
Currency: Pataca
Exports: Clothing, textiles, footwear, toys, electrical and electronic equipment.

Portuguese explorers established Macau as a trading and missionary post in 1537, and Portugal leased it from China in 1557. Macau was annexed in 1849 and, from 1887, was recognized by the Chinese government as a Portuguese colony, which it remained until it reverted to China in 1974 (although Macau remained under Portuguese administration until 1999). Macau is a special administrative region of China. The flag depicts, on a green field, a three-leafed lotus flower representing the islands of Macau. A stylized bridge and water indicate the inseparable contact with mainland China, while the golden colour of the five stars is derived from the Chinese flag.

TAIWAN

Republic of China

Flag proportions: 2:3
Adopted: 28 October 1928
Capital: Taipei
Area: 36,179km² (13,969sq mi)
Population: 22,790,000
Language: Chinese (Mandarin), Min, Hakka

Religion: Chinese folk religion (including Daoism), Buddhism
Currency: Taiwan dollar
Exports: Computers and computer products, electrical equipment, metals, textiles, plastics, synthetic fibres.

The Taiwanese flag was the national flag of China from 1928–49, when Chiang Kai-Shek's Chinese Nationalist Party, or Kuomintang, was in power. After the communist victory in 1949, the nationalists retreated to Formosa (now Taiwan) and established a government based on China's pre-1947 constitution. The white sun on a blue field is the flag of the Kuomintang. The blue background stands for liberty and justice; the sun represents equality and light, with the 12 rays representing the hours of the clock, against which progress is constantly measured. The red field is for brotherhood, sacrifice and the Han Chinese, the dominant race in China.

MONGOLIA

Mongolia

Flag proportions: 1:2
Adopted: 12 February 1992
Capital: Ulan Bator (Ulaanbaatar)
Area: 1,564,100 km²
(603,905sq mi)
Population: 2,504,000
Language: Khalka Mongolian,

Kazakh
Religion: Tantric Buddhism
(Lamaism), non-religious
Currency: Tugrik
Exports: Mineral products
(particularly copper), live animals,
textiles, animal products, flourspar.

Three vertical bands of red, blue, red have been used on the Mongolian flag since 1940, when the *soyombo*, the country's national emblem, was added at the hoist. The uppermost symbol is a flame above a sun and crescent moon. Inverted triangles are ancient Mongol symbols for death. Horizontal panels indicate watchfulness, as do the two stylized fish which make up the Chinese yin–yang symbol. Two vertical columns express the old proverb that 'the friendship of two men is stronger than stone walls'. A star surmounting the emblem was removed in 1992 and the design of the *soyombo* was modified.

JAPAN

Japan

Flag proportions: 7:10
Adopted: 13 August 1999
Capital: Tokyo
Area: 377,819km²
(145,887sq mi)
Population: 127,806,000
Language: Japanese
Religion: Buddhism,

Shinto traditions
Currency: Yen
Exports: Motor vehicles, electrical
and electronic equipment, office
machinery, chemicals, scientific
and optical equipment, iron and
steel products.

The red *Hinomaru* or 'disc of the sun' recalls the worship of Amaterasu Omikami, the Sun Goddess of the Shinto faith. The present national flag, with a red disc on a white field, was adopted after the restoration of the Meiji dynasty and the inauguration of Emperor Mutsuhito in 1867, which introduced an era of rapid change and westernization. The white field denotes purity and honesty, while red is said to stand for warmth and sincerity. Although Japan is known as the 'Land of the Rising Sun', the Japanese national flag has never depicted the sun with rays.

NORTH KOREA

Democratic People's Republic of Korea

Flag proportions: 1:2
Adopted: 9 September 1948
Capital: Pyongyang
Area: 122,762km² (47,399sq mi)
Population: 22,224,000
Language: Korean

Religion: Non-religious, traditional beliefs, Chondogyo
Currency: Won
Exports: Minerals, metallurgical products, armaments, textiles, fishery products.

From 1910 the flag of Japan flew over the annexed Korean peninsula. In 1948, the former kingdom was partitioned along latitude 38° North (the 38th parallel) into a communist north and democratic south. The flag adopted by North Korea expressed its newly acquired communist ideology with a five-pointed red star on a white disc, situated on a broad, horizontal red band bordered above and below by a narrow white stripe and a broader blue stripe. The flag retains the traditional Korean colours, with special prominence given to red, for the communist revolution. The white disc recalls the Chinese yin–yang symbol.

SOUTH KOREA

The Republic of Korea

Flag proportions: 2:3
Adopted: October 1997
Capital: Seoul
Area: 99,461km² (38,402sq mi)
Population: 47,279,000
Language: Korean
Religion: Non-religious, Buddhist,

various Protestant churches
Currency: Won
Exports: Electronics, machinery and transport equipment (including motor vehicles), computers, steel, ships, textiles, clothing, footwear.

The basic design of Korea's national flag was re-established after Korea was liberated from Japanese rule in 1945, and there have been minor modifications since then. White represents peace and purity, and is also Korea's traditional colour. At the flag's centre is the yin-yang symbol. The four groups of black bars, or trigrams, derive from the *I-Ching* (Book of Changes), a Chinese divination system. The pattern of broken (yin) and unbroken (yang) bars illustrates principles of movement and harmony. The three intact trigrams (top left) represent heaven. Moving clockwise, the other trigrams in turn depict water, earth and fire.

North Korea, South Korea and the DMZ

Following the failure of the Japanese occupation in 1945, the Korean Peninsula was divided arbitrarily along the 38th parallel (38° North) into zones of temporary occupation, with the USA controlling the south and the Soviet Union the north. In 1948 this unnatural division was made permanent with the founding of the separate states of North Korea and South Korea.

The heavily mechanized, communist-led northern army invaded the south in 1950, resulting in a US-led military response by the United Nations. The war ended inconclusively in 1953, following which a demilitarized zone (DMZ) some 4km (2.5 miles) wide was created between the two countries which, having signed no peace treaty, are technically still at war.

Tension along the DMZ has always been high, and has impacted upon diplomatic relations between the two Koreas. The situation is not helped by North Korea's nuclear capabilities, coupled with the country's fast-declining economy, chronic food shortages and extensive armed forces.

However, although their governments have been hostile for more than five decades, the common people of both North Korea and South Korea have expressed a strong desire for the reunification of the peninsula by flying a single flag. Dating back to at least 1989, the flag is white with a representation in blue silhouette of the Korean peninsula.

VIETNAM

The Socialist Republic of Vietnam

Flag proportions: 2:3
Adopted: 30 November 1955
Capital: Hanoi (Ha Nôi)
Area: 329,315km² (127,150sq mi)
Population: 83,120,000
Language: Vietnamese

Religion: Buddhist, non-religious, Roman Catholic
Currency: Dong
Exports: Crude petroleum, fish and fish products, coffee, rice, rubber, tea, clothing, footwear.

Vietnam was part of French Indochina when Japan invaded in 1940. Following Japan's defeat, Vietnamese nationalists fought against the restoration of French colonial rule. In 1954, under the Geneva Convention, Vietnam was divided into communist North and pro-Western South, resulting in the Vietnam War (1964–76). After Saigon's fall, the country was united as the Socialist Republic of Vietnam, under the flag of North Vietnam. The flag consists of a five-pointed gold star at the centre of a red field. The points of the star represent the unity of the five groups of workers who built socialism. Red stands for revolution, and also for the blood shed by the Vietnamese people.

LAOS

Lao People's Democratic Republic

Flag proportions: 2:3
Adopted: 2 December 1975
Capital: Vientiane (Viangchan)
Area: 236,800km²
(91,429sq mi)
Population: 5,610,000

Language: Lao, Khmer
Religion: Buddhist, traditional beliefs
Currency: Kip
Exports: Garments, wood products, coffee, electricity, tin.

Laos gained independence from France in 1953 and became a communist state in 1975, when the present national flag was introduced. The flag is divided into a broad horizontal blue band at the centre, flanked top and bottom by a red band. Red is for the blood shed in the struggle for freedom during the civil war (1953–75), and blue is for wealth. The white disc symbolizes the ruling Lao People's Revolutionary Party leading the country to prosperity. The disc is said to be based on the one in the Japanese national flag, used in recognition of Japan's work against western colonialism.

CAMBODIA

The Kingdom of Cambodia

Flag proportions: 2:3
Adopted: 30 June 1993
Capital: Phnom Penh
Area: 181,035km²
(69,898sq mi)
Population: 13,807,000

Language: Khmer
Religion: Buddhist
Currency: Riel
Exports: Clothing, logs and sawn timber, rubber, rice, fish, tobacco, footwear.

Cambodia became a French protectorate in 1863. During most of World War II the country was occupied by Japan. Part of Indochina, Cambodia raised its own flag in 1949 when it achieved semi-autonomy from France, before becoming independent in 1953. The present flag, dating from 1948, was reintroduced when the monarchy was reinstated in 1993, several other versions having been flown in the interim. The ancient temple of Angkor Wat, revered as the sanctuary of the Lord Creator of the world, is depicted in the red band. The temple buildings rest on a pedestal, representing the structure of the universe.

MYANMAR (BURMA)

Union of Myanmar

Flag proportions: 5:9
Adopted: 4 January 1974
Capital: Naypyidaw
Area: 676,577km²
(261,228sq mi)
Population: 49,008,000
Language: Burmese, Shan, Karen, Arakanese (Rakhine)

Religion: Buddhist
Currency: Kyat
Exports: Clothing, natural gas, wood and wood products, food and live animals, materials (including gypsum and precious stones).

Burma became the Union of Myanmar in 1989, adopting a flag as a symbol of resistance to Japanese occupation in World War II. Burma was a British colony until 1948, when it achieved independence. The flag (a white star on a red field) was modified by the addition of a blue canton and five small stars. The present design features 14 stars enclosing a 14-toothed pinion and ears of rice, representing industry and agriculture respectively. Fourteen corresponds to the number of states in the country, and the stars represent unity between them. Red signifies courage and decisiveness, white is for purity and blue is for peace and integrity.

THAILAND

Kingdom of Thailand

Flag proportions: 2:3
Adopted: 28 September 1917
Capital: Bangkok (Krung Thep)
Area: 513,115km²
(198,114sq mi)
Population: 62,800,000
Language: Thai, Lao, Chinese

Religion: Buddhist
Currency: Baht
Exports: Computer and office machinery, other electrical and non-electrical machinery, rubber, motor vehicles, plastics, seafood and live fish, clothing.

Thailand's flag was originally an expression of support for the Allied cause in World War I (most Allied flags used red, white and blue). The field is divided into horizontal bands, with the central blue band being one third of the depth of the flag. The bands of white and red above and below are each one sixth of the flag's depth. The colours symbolize the lifeblood of the country (red), the purity of the people and their Buddhist faith (white), and the monarchy (blue). The Thai people are proud of their culture and their flag, which is widely displayed.

MALAYSIA

Malaysia

Flag proportions: 1:2
Adopted: 16 September 1963
Capital: Kuala Lumpur (legislative capital), Putrajaya (administrative capital)
Area: 329,847km² (127,355sq mi)
Population: 26,128,000
Language: Malay, English, Chinese, Tamil

Religion: Sunni Islam, Buddhist, Chinese folk religions (including Daoism)
Currency: Ringgit
Exports: Electronic equipment, machinery, transport equipment petroleum and petroleum products, wood and wood products, rubber, textiles, chemicals.

When Malaya changed its name to Malaysia in 1963, it adopted a flag closely resembling the US Stars and Stripes, with Islamic symbols. The seven red and seven white stripes symbolize unity within the federation, as do the 14 rays (points of the star) in the chief canton. The crescent and star together represent Islam, the principal religion. Blue represents Malaysian unity. Yellow, the colour of the crescent and the star, is the traditional colour of Malaysian rulers. Malaysia comprises 13 states and three federal territories: Kuala Lumpur, Labuan and Putrajaya.

SINGAPORE

Republic of Singapore

Flag proportions: 2:3
Adopted: 3 December 1959
Capital: Singapore (Hsin-chia-p'o) (Singapura)
Area: 697km² (269sq mi)
Population: 4,484,000
Languages: Chinese,

Malay, English
Religion: Buddhist, Chinese folk religions, Sunni Islam
Currency: Singaporean dollar
Exports: Machinery, transport equipment, consumer goods, chemicals, petroleum products.

Singapore was leased to the British East India Company in 1819. The flag was first used when Singapore received self-government from Britain in 1959, retained when it joined the Malaysian Federation in 1963 and formally adopted when the country gained independence within the Commonwealth in 1965. The flag is horizontally divided into equal bands of red over white, colours associated with the Malay people. Red represents equality and universal brotherhood, while white stands for virtue and purity. The white crescent signifies that Singapore is a new and growing nation. The five five-pointed stars stand for equality, justice, democracy, peace and progress.

BRUNEI

Brunei Darussalam

Flag proportions: 1:2
Adopted: 29 September 1959
Capital: Bandar Seri Begawan
Area: 5,765km² (2,226sq mi)
Population: 358,000

Language: Malay, Chinese
Religion: Sunni Islam, Buddhist
Currency: Brunei dollar
Exports: Crude petroleum, natural gas, petroleum products.

Brunei is an absolute monarchy. The principal flag colour, yellow, is associated with the ruling Sultan, while the angled bands of black and white represent his chief ministers. At the centre of the flag is the state coat of arms in red. The twin-tailed flag and umbrella are royal symbols, while the upturned crescent represents Islam. The hands signify government protection and promotion of the people's rights. Two four-feathered wings symbolize the protection of justice, peace, tranquility and prosperity. The Arabic motto on the crescent translates as 'Always render service by the guidance of Allah', while the inscription on the scroll beneath it reads 'Brunei City of Peace'.

PHILIPPINES

Republic of the Philippines

Flag proportions: 1:2
Adopted: 16 September 1997
Capital: Manila
Area: 300,076km² (115,860sq mi)
Population: 88,706,000
Language: Pilipino (Filipino or Tagalog), English, Cebuano, Ilocano
Religion: Roman Catholic,

Sunni Islam
Currency: Philippine Peso
Exports: Electronic equipment (particularly computer peripherals), machinery and transport equipment, clothing, coconut oil, chemicals, wiring.

When the Philippines gained independence from the USA in 1946, the flag raised had originally been used by nationalists during the struggle for freedom from Spain. The white triangle represents peace and purity, red is for courage, and blue is for honour and ideals (patriotism). Within the triangle are an eight-rayed sun and three stars, all in gold. The stars represent the Philippine's main regions (Luzon, Visayas, Mindanao) while the sun stands for liberty, and represents the eight provinces that revolted against Spain.

INDONESIA

Republic of Indonesia

Flag proportions: 2:3
Adopted: 17 August 1945
Capital: Jakarta
Area: 1,904,413km² (735,309sq mi)
Population: 222,192,000
Language: Bahasa Indonesia
(Indonesian Malay), Javanese,

Sundanese, Madurese
Religion: Sunni Islam
Currency: Indonesian Rupiah
Exports: Crude petroleum and
natural gas, electrical goods,
plywood, processed rubber,
textiles, clothing.

Indonesia was a Dutch colony from 1816 until 1945, when independence was proclaimed (it was not recognized by the Dutch until 1949). The government of 1945 was encouraged by Japanese opposition to Western colonialism, and based the flag on colours used by a 13th-century Indonesian empire. It comprises equal horizontal bands of red above white, sacred colours of the ancient empire, which were deliberately chosen by the nationalist movement of the 1940s. Officially called *Sang Dwiwarna* (exalted bicolour), the flag symbolizes the complete person: red for the body and physical life, and white for the soul and spiritual existence.

EAST TIMOR

Democratic Republic of Timor-Leste

Flag proportions: 2:3
Adopted: 20 May 2002
Capital: Dili
Area: 14,874km² (5,743sq mi)
Population: 923,000

Language: Portuguese, Tetum
Religion: Roman Catholic
Currency: US dollar
Exports: Timber (sandlewood),
coffee, marble, natural gas.

East Timor became independent from Indonesia in May 2002, when the flag of an interim UN administration was replaced with a flag dating from the country's 1975 transition from Portuguese colony to independent state (ended by an invasion by pro-Indonesian militias). The black triangle represents periods of colonization, which endured for about 400 years. The yellow chevron depicts the struggle for independence and the hope of prosperity. Red is for the blood shed for independence, a poignant association in view of the mass murders committed upon the East Timorese in 1999. White is for peace, and the five-pointed star is a light of hope for the nation's future.

CHRISTMAS ISLAND

Territory of Christmas Island

Flag proportions: 1:2
Adopted: 2002
Capital: The Settlement
Area: 135km² (52sq mi)
Population: 1,500
Language: English, Chinese

Religion: Buddhism, Chinese folk
religions (including Daoism),
Sunni Islam
Currency: Australian dollar
Exports: Phosphate

Depending on phosphate workings staffed by Chinese and Malay migrants, Christmas Island is an isolated mountainous island south of Java (Indonesia). Annexed by Great Britain in 1888, the island was transferred to Australian rule in 1958. The island flag is blue and green, representing the sea and the land. It displays the Australian Southern Cross in white on blue, an outline of the island in green in the gold central disc, and the endemic Golden Bosun bird in gold on green.

COCOS (KEELING) ISLANDS

Territory of the Cocos (Keeling) Islands

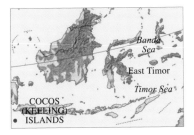

Flag proportions: 1:2
Adopted: 2003 (in public use although not formally adopted)
Capital: Bantam Village
Area: 14km² (6sq mi)
Population: 620

Language: English, Malay
Religion: Sunni Islam
Currency: Australian dollar
Exports: Coconuts and coconut products (copra).

The Cocos (Keeling) Islands are small coral islands, southwest of Indonesia. The (British) Clunies Ross family established palm-tree plantations in 1826, and were recognized as rulers by the British government in 1886. In 1955, Britain ceded the islands to Australia, which purchased the rights of the Clunies Ross family in 1978. The official flag of the islands is that of Australia. However, on the islands themselves, a green flag displaying the Australian Southern Cross, the cresent moon of the majority Malay Muslim population, and a palm tree, all in gold, is flown.

AUSTRALIA, NEW ZEALAND AND OCEANIA

Australia, the world's smallest continent, has an area of 7.68 million km², but is also the greatest landmass of the territories of the Indo-Pacific region collectively known as Australasia and Oceania. Before European settlement, perhaps a few hundred thousand native Australians or Aborigines lived here.

To the north of Australia are the East Indies – the trade-route islands of silks and spices. The mix of peoples is complex, deriving in part from the Asian mainland and the island groups of Polynesia, Melanesia and Micronesia. History and ethnicity are reflected in flags that carry, among other emblems, a pig's tusk and the Union Flag of Great Britain.

Most settlement patterns were established centuries ago by indigenous or near-indigenous peoples who crossed immense distances of ocean in open boats. The Maori, a Polynesian people, settled New Zealand from the 10th century onwards. By contrast, the many Australians of Asian origin are much more recent, as a 'white Australia'

immigration policy was abandoned only in the 1960s. World War II resulted in a long-lasting American influence, most directly in the former United States Trust Territory of the Pacific Islands. Subsequent treaties include ANZUS (a defence pact involving Australia, New Zealand and the USA), and the South Pacific Forum, a political and economic association of some 15 states, with its headquarters in Fiji.

During the past 50 years Australia's economy has transformed: 75 per cent of export earnings in 1947 were derived from agriculture, but farm-based earnings are nearer to 20 per cent while the mining and manufacturing sectors have advanced. New Zealand's economy is based on agriculture, although the industrial sector is growing. Deposits of oil and minerals occur throughout Oceania, as in Papua New Guinea, which also exports rubber, timber and tropical fruits. Cruise liners carrying tourists among the islands are an important source of foreign revenue for the smaller states and dependencies.

AT A GLANCE

Biggest country: Australia
Smallest country: Nauru
Largest city: Sydney, Australia
Major cities: Auckland, Adelaide, Brisbane, Christchurch, Melbourne, Perth, Wellington.

Highestpoint: Mt Wilhelm, Papua New Guinea – 4,509m (14,794ft).
Lowest point: Lake Eyre, Australia 16m (52ft) below sea level).
Longest river: Murray-Darling, Australia – 3,750km (2,330mi).

Australia, New Zealand and Oceania

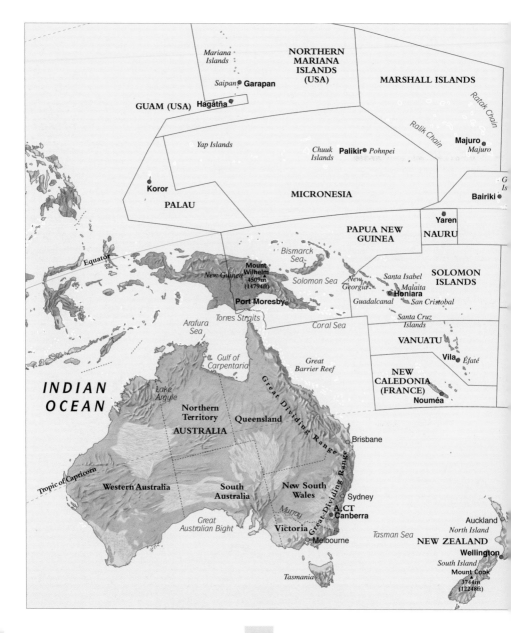

Mariana
Islands

**NORTHERN
MARIANA
ISLANDS
(USA)**

Saipan● **Garapan**

MARSHALL ISLANDS

Ratak Chain

GUAM (USA) **Hagåtña**●

Ralik Chain

Yap Islands

Chuuk **Palikir**● Pohnpei
Islands

Majuro ●
Majuro

●
Koror

MICRONESIA

G
Is
Bairiki ●

PALAU

Yaren

**PAPUA NEW
GUINEA**

NAURU

Bismarck
Sea

Equator

Mount
Wilhelm
New Guinea 4509m
(14794ft)

Solomon Sea

New
Georgia

Santa Isabel

Malaita

**SOLOMON
ISLANDS**

●**Honiara**

Port Moresby●

Guadalcanal

San Cristobal

Arafura
Sea

Torres Straits

Coral Sea

Santa Cruz
Islands

VANUATU

Gulf of
Carpentaria

Great
Barrier Reef

Vila● Éfaté

**NEW
CALEDONIA
(FRANCE)**

***INDIAN
OCEAN***

Lake
Argyle

Northern
Territory

Queensland

Great Dividing Range

Nouméa

AUSTRALIA

Brisbane

Tropic of Capricorn

Western Australia

South
Australia

New South
Wales

Sydney

Murray

A.CT
●**Canberra**

Auckland

Great
Australian Bight

Victoria

Melbourne

Tasman Sea

North Island

NEW ZEALAND

Wellington

South Island
Mount Cook
▲
3744m
(12248ft)

Tasmania

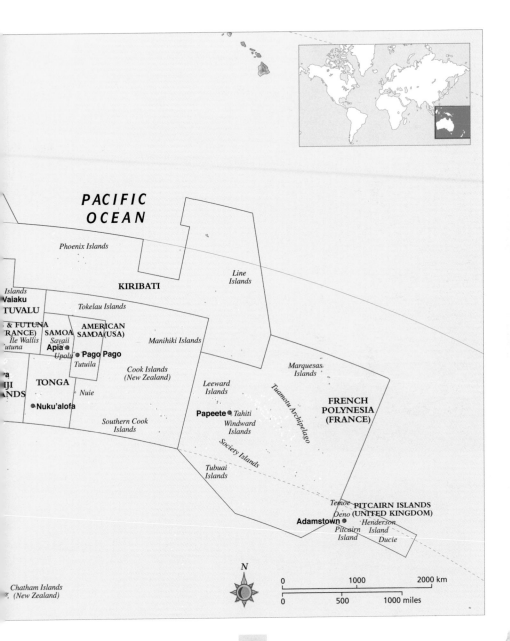

*PACIFIC
OCEAN*

Phoenix Islands

*Line
Islands*

KIRIBATI

Islands
Vaiaku
TUVALU

Tokelau Islands

& FUTUNA
RANCE) **SAMOA** **AMERICAN**
Île Wallis *Savaii* **SAMOA (USA)**
'utuna **Apia**
Upolu ● **Pago Pago**
Tutuila

Manihiki Islands

*Cook Islands
(New Zealand)*

*Marquesas
Islands*

a
IJI
NDS
TONGA
Nuie

*Leeward
Islands*

**FRENCH
POLYNESIA
(FRANCE)**

● **Nuku'alofa**

*Southern Cook
Islands*

Papeete ● *Tahiti*
*Windward
Islands*

Tuamotu Archipelago

Society Islands

*Tubuai
Islands*

Temoe **PITCAIRN ISLANDS**
Oeno **(UNITED KINGDOM)**
Adamstown ● *Henderson
Pitcairn Island
Island* *Ducie*

N

*Chatham Islands
F. (New Zealand)*

0	1000	2000 km
0	500	1000 miles

NORTHERN MARIANA ISLANDS

Commonwealth of the Northern
Mariana Islands

Flag proportions: 20:39
Adopted: 25 October 1988
Capital: Garapan (on Saipan)
Area: 477km² (184sq mi)
Population: 69,000

Language: English, Chamorro
Religion: Roman Catholic
Currency: US dollar
Exports: Clothing, agriculture and
fishing products.

The Northern Mariana Islands, a self-governing incorporated US territory, form part (with Guam) of the Marianas archipelago in the northwest Pacific. Raised in 1976, the flag has a white star in the centre of a blue field, typifying the Pacific Ocean, which surrounds the islands with security and love. The star represents the islands that make up the US Commonwealth territories. It is set upon a grey *latte* stone, symbolizing the culture of the Chamorro people. In 1989 a wreath of flowers and shells was placed to encircle the original design. This wreath, comprising ylang-ylang, *seyur*, *ang'gha* and *teibwo* flowers, is another symbol of indigenous culture.

AUSTRALIA

Commonwealth of Australia

Flag proportions: 1:2
Adopted: 15 April 1954
Capital: Canberra
Area: 7,703,429km²
(2,974,320sq mi)
Population: 19,855,000
Language: English

Religion: Roman Catholic,
Anglican
Currency: Australian dollar
Exports: Coal, gold, meat, wool,
iron ore and other metallic ores
including alumina, wheat,
machinery, transport equipment.

Australia flies a version of the British Blue Ensign, with the Union Flag in the chief canton. The Southern Cross, a prominent southern constellation, is depicted at the fly. The large Commonwealth Star beneath the Union Flag represents the six states, Northern Territory and the external territories administered by the federal government.

The British flag was first flown on Australian soil by the explorer Captain James Cook in 1778, and remained the official flag until 1954, after which the present Australian flag, which had previously flown alongside the Union Flag, was flown alone.

Australian State Flags

All state flags, other than those of the Northern Territory and the federal capital, Canberra (situated in the Australian Capital Territory, or ACT), are based on the Blue Ensign and charged with the state badge in the fly. Some predate the national flag.

The Northern Territory flag uses black and ochre to symbolize its Aboriginal heritage and desert environment. The ACT flag depicts Canberra's coat of arms alongside the Southern Cross in the city colours of gold and blue.

Australian Capital Territory
1993

Tasmania
1975

Queensland
1959

Victoria
1901

South Australia
1904

Western Australia
1954

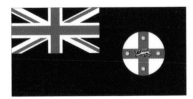

New South Wales
1876

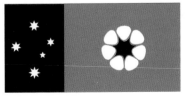

Northern Territory
1978

GUAM

Guam

Flag proportions: 22:41
Adopted: 9 February 1948
Capital: Hagatna
Area: 541km² (209sq mi)
Population: 155,000
Language: English, Chamorro,

Filipino
Religion: Roman Catholic
Currency: US dollar
Exports: Re-exported petroleum, construction materials, foodstuffs, fish.

Guam, the largest of the Mariana Islands, is an unincorporated US territory and a major naval and air base. It was ceded to the US by Spain in 1898. The flag was designed in 1917 by the wife of an American naval officer, and the red border was added in 1948. By tradition, it is flown together with the US flag. The deep blue field represents the Pacific Ocean. The central oval shape, edged with red, is said to represent the slingshots used by the Chamorro people for hunting and warfare. Within the oval is a depiction of a coconut palm. The tree, at the mouth of the Agaña River, has survived several typhoons and denotes tenacity and courage. The boat is a *proa*, a fast seagoing canoe that symbolizes courage and enterprise.

PALAU

The Republic of Palau

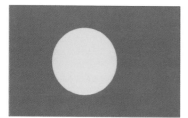

Flag proportions: 3:5
Adopted: 1 January 1981
Capital: Melekeok
Area: 458km² (177sq mi)
Population: 19,900
Language: Palauan, English,

Filipino
Religion: Roman Catholic, Modekngei
Currency: US dollar
Exports: Shellfish, tuna, copra, clothing.

When Palau became a republic in 1981, it adopted a flag with a simple design suggesting a full moon on the water or in the sky. However, when explained in terms of Palauan culture, the blue field is neither sea nor sky but represents the transition from foreign domination to independence and the freedom of self-rule. The gold disc is set slightly towards the hoist, and does indeed represent the moon, because a full moon is regarded as the most favourable time for celebrations, planting or harvesting. It also signifies tranquillity, peace and love. Before independence, Palau was part of the US Trust Territory of the Pacific Islands, and flew a version of the flag of the Federated States of Micronesia.

MICRONESIA

Federated States of Micronesia

Flag proportions: 1:2
Adopted: 30 November 1978
Capital: Palikir
Area: 701km² (271sq mi)
Population: 108,000
Language: English, Chuukese,

Pohnpeian, Mortlockese
Religion: Roman Catholic,
Congregational
Currency: US dollar
Exports: Fish, clothing, bananas,
black pepper.

Situated in the northwest of Oceania, the Federated States of Micronesia are a collection of islands in the Caroline group. Prior to independence in 1986, they were part of the US-administered United States Trust Territory of the Pacific Islands. The darker blue of the Micronesian flag represents the Pacific Ocean. Four white stars are arranged as a cross, each star representing an island state that makes up the federation, namely Chuuk, Kosrae, Pohnpei and Yap. (Two of the original six Trust Territories, Palau and the Marshall Islands, opted for separate independence.) Each state has its own flag, comprising a blue field charged with the state emblem.

MARSHALL ISLANDS

The Republic of the Marshall Islands

Flag proportions: 10:19
Adopted: 1 May 1979
Capital: Majuro
Area: 181km² (70sq mi)
Population: 51,000

Language: Marshallese
Religion: Congregational
Currency: US dollar
Exports: Copra, coconut oil,
handicrafts, fish.

The long arms of the white star in the chief canton are said to depict a Christian cross, while the 24 points represent the Marshall Islands' municipalities. The twin stripes represent the parallel island chains of Ratak (sunrise, white) and Ralik (sunset, orange). The stripes widen and rise towards the fly, signifying growth and vitality. White is for peace and orange symbolizes prosperity and courage. Another interpretation is that the star and rising stripes depict the islands' position a few degrees north of the Equator. The dark blue field depicts the Pacific Ocean, across which the islands are scattered.

PAPUA NEW GUINEA

The Independent State of Papua
New Guinea

Flag proportions: 3:4
Adopted: 1 July 1971
Capital: Port Moresby
Area: 462,840km²
(178,704sq mi)
Population: 5,191,000
Language: English, Tok Pisin
(Pidgin English), 817 other

local languages
Religion: Traditional beliefs,
Roman Catholic, Lutheran
Currency: Kina
Exports: Petroleum, gold, copper,
timber, coffee, cocoa, crayfish,
prawns.

The flag of Papua New Guinea (PNG) was designed by a local teacher, who chose red and black because of the colours' widespread use in the country's indigenous art. The field comprises two right-angled triangles descending diagonally from the top of the hoist. The upper red triangle depicts, in gold, the *kumul* (bird of paradise) in flight, whose feathers were once used for ornamenting traditional headdresses. In the black triangle, five stars represent the Southern Cross as it appears over PNG, and also refer to a legend about five sisters.

NAURU

The Republic of Nauru

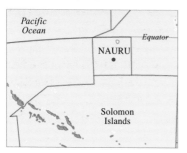

Flag proportions: 1:2
Adopted: 31 January 1968
Capital: Yaren (although never
officially proclaimed)
Area: 21.3km² (8sq mi)
Population: 10,100

Language: Nauruan, English,
Kiribati
Religion: Congregational, Roman
Catholic
Currency: Australian dollar
Exports: Phosphates.

The royal blue field, symbolizing clear skies and a calm ocean, is divided by a horizontal gold stripe, representing the equator. The 12-pointed white star stands for the indigenous tribes of Nauru. The position of the star reflects the island's position one degree south of the equator. Europeans first visited the island in 1798. Part of the German Empire from 1888, it came under Australian administration after 1918. During World War II the Japanese destroyed the mining facilities and deported much of the population to Truk Atoll. Nauru was a UN trust territory, jointly administered by Australia, New Zealand and the UK, from 1947 until independence in 1968.

SOLOMON ISLANDS

Solomon Islands

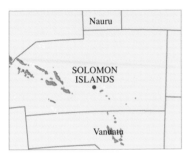

Flag proportions: 1:2
Adopted: 18 November 1977
Capital: Honiara
Area: 28,370km² (10,954sq mi)
Population: 495,000
Language: English, various

Melanesian languages
Religion: Anglican, Roman
Catholic, Potestant Evangelical
Currency: Solomon Islands dollar
Exports: Timber products, fish,
palm oil, copra, cocoa.

The Solomons comprise hundreds of islands in the Melanesian archipelago, including Guadalcanal (the largest), Malaita, San Cristobal, New Georgia and Santa Isabela. First sighted by Europeans in 1568, they became a British colony in 1883. Self-government was granted in 1976, and independence within the Commonwealth in 1978.

The five five-pointed white stars stand for the five main groups of islands of this constitutional monarchy. The diagonal yellow stripe represents sunshine, while the blue and green triangles represent the sea and land. Japan occupied the Solomons for much of World War II.

VANUATU

The Republic of Vanuatu

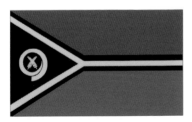

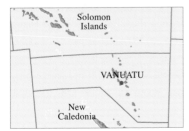

Flag proportions: 3:5
Adopted: 30 July 1980
Capital: Port-Vila
Area: 12,190km² (4,707sq mi)
Population: 195,000
Languages: Bislama (English

Creole) English, French
Religion: Presbyterian, traditional
beliefs, Roman Catholic, Anglican
Currency: Vatu
Exports: Copra, beef, veal, timber,
cocoa, coffee.

The golden Y-shape depicts the layout of the 70 islands of the Vanuatu archipelago. Gold is for sunshine, black is for the indigenous Melanesians, green is for natural wealth and red is for striving and sacrifice. A gold object set in the black triangle depicts a curled boar's tusk, a symbol of prosperity. Within the curve of the tusk are two crossed *namele* ferns, representing peace. Europeans reached the islands in 1606, calling them the New Hebrides. Jointly administered by Britain and France from 1906, they escaped occupation by Japan in World War II. In 1980 the New Hebrides became Vanuatu, an independent republic within the Commonwealth.

NEW CALEDONIA

Territory of New Caledonia and Dependencies

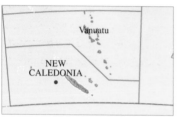

Flag proportions: 2:3
Adopted: n/a
Capital: Nouméa
Area: 18,576km² (7,172sq mi)
Population: 231,000

Languages: French, Derhu
Religion: Roman Catholic
Currency: French Pacific franc
Exports: Refined ferro-nickel and nickel, nickel ore, fish.

An overseas territory of France, this group of islands, 1,400km (870mi) northeast of Brisbane, was settled by both Britain and France during the first half of the 19th century. It became a French possession in 1853, and served as a penal colony from 1864 until the early 20th century.

The status of the territory makes it legal for an approved flag to be flown alongside the *Tricolore*, but not on its own. The current local choice consists of a red field upon which is depicted, in white, the flightless crane-like bird, known locally as a *cagou*, which occurs only in New Caledonia.

TUVALU

The Constitutional Monarchy of Tuvalu

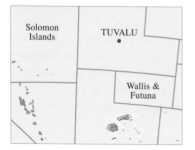

Flag proportions: 1:2
Adopted: 11 April 1997
Capital: Vaiaku on Fongafale islet
Area: 24km² (9sq mi)
Population: 9,600
Languages: Tuvaluan, English

Religion: Congregational Church of Tuvalu
Currency: Tuvalu dollar (local issue of the Australian dollar)
Exports: Copra, fish, clothing, fruit, vegetables.

Tuvalu flies a light blue version of the British Blue Ensign, perhaps to represent the clear waters of the Pacific Ocean. The nine five-pointed yellow stars represent the islands of the archipelago. When flying from a flagpole, with the fly pointing north, the stars on the flag are seen to be occupying the geographical positions of the islands. First reached by Europeans in 1795, the islands were a source of slave labour in the mid-19th century. A British protectorate from 1892, Tuvalu was part of the Gilbert and Ellice Islands from 1915–75, when the two groups separated to become Kiribati and Tuvalu. Independence within the Commonwealth came in 1978.

WALLIS AND FUTUNA

Wallis and Futuna Islands

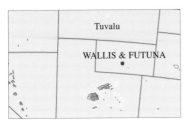

Flag proportions: 2:3
Adopted: 5 March 1848
Capital: Mata-Utu
Area: 274km² (106sq mi)
Population: 15,000
Languages: French, Wallisian,
Futunian
Religion: Roman Catholic
Currency: French Pacific franc
Exports: Copra, coconuts,
chemicals, construction materials.

Wallis and Futuna is a French Overseas Territory, so the flag may only be displayed with the *Tricolore*. The white emblem on the red field is made up of four triangles with each base parallel to an edge and the apex at the centre. Three triangles represent three hereditary rulers, while the fourth denotes French sovereignty over this autonomous territory. The emblem was probably introduced by French missionaries and retained when the islands became a protectorate in 1842. A white-bordered *Tricolore* occupies the chief canton. Red symbolizes courage, white the purity of high ideals.

FIJI

Sovereign Democratic Republic of the Fiji Islands

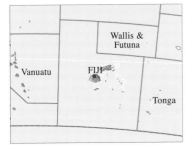

Flag proportions: 1:2
Adopted: 10 October 1970
Capital: Suva
Area: 18,272km² (7,055sq mi)
Population: 828,000
Language: English, Fijian, Hindi
Religion: Hindu, Methodist,
Roman Catholic
Currency: Fiji dollar
Exports: Sugar, clothing, gold,
fish, timber, molasses, coconuts.

Originally inhabited by Melanesian and Polynesian people, Fiji became a British crown colony in 1874. It achieved independence within the Commonwealth in 1970, and then became a republic in 1987. The Fijian flag, one of the first to adopt a Blue Ensign with light blue, uses that colour to distinguish it from Australia and New Zealand's flags. The Union Flag is in the chief canton, with the shield from the republic's coat of arms at the fly. On the chief (the top third of the shield) is a crowned lion. Below the chief, the shield is quartered by St George's cross on a white field. The quarters show sugar cane, a coconut palm, a dove of peace and a bunch of bananas.

TONGA

Kingdom of Tonga

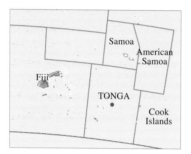

Flag proportions: 1:2
Adopted: 4 November 1875
Capital: Nuku'alofa
Area: 748km² (289sq mi)
Population: 101,000
Language: Tongan

Religion: Free Wesleyan
Methodist, Roman Catholic,
Mormon
Currency: Pa'anga
Exports: Squash, fish, vanilla
beans, root crops.

In 1862, King George Tupou I commanded that his country's flag should symbolize the Christian faith. The flag was thus conceived to be red with a red cross on a white canton. The king encouraged the spread of Christianity, and the 1875 constitution states that the flag should be used for all time. Red is for Christ's blood, white is for purity, and the cross is a Christian symbol. A British protectorate from 1900, Tonga achieved independence as an hereditary monarchy within the Commonwealth in 1970. Early European visitors included Abel Tasman in 1643, but it was Captain Cook who bestowed the title, 'The Friendly Islands', in 1773. Out of about 170 islands, only 36 are inhabited.

SAMOA

The Independent State of Samoa

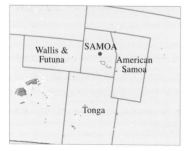

Flag proportions: 1:2
Adopted: 26 April 1949
Capital: Apia
Area: 2,831km² (1,093sq mi)
Population: 179,000
Language: Samoan

Religion: Mormon,
Congregational, Roman Catholic
Currency: Tala
Exports: Fish, coconut oil,
coconut cream, copra, automobile
parts, clothing, beer.

The flag, granted in 1948 when Samoa was a territory of New Zealand, was jointly created by the kings of the rival kingdoms of Malietoa and Tamasese. It combined elements of their flags with the four-star Southern Cross of New Zealand, which appears in the chief canton. A small fifth star was added in 1949, making the constellation more like that of Australia. White stars stand for purity, while the blue background denotes freedom. Red is for courage. In 1962, Samoa (formerly Western Samoa) became the first Polynesian nation to be granted independence, as a constitutional monarchy within the Commonwealth. There are two main islands, Savai'i and Upolu, and two smaller islands.

AMERICAN SAMOA

American Samoa

Flag proportions: 10:19
Adopted: 17 April 1960
Capital: Pago Pago
Area: 199km² (77sq mi)
Population: 57,000
Language: Samoan, English

Religion: Congregational, Roman Catholic
Currency: US dollar
Exports: Tuna.

The flag is blue with an isosceles triangle based on the fly, its red-edged equal sides extending to a point midway along the hoist. At the fly is a 'proper' American bald eagle in flight. Its left claw clasps a staff, a symbol of Samoan nobility and wisdom. In the eagle's right claw is a club used in ritual dances, representing the power of the chiefs. The symbolism of America's national bird clasping traditional icons of Samoan authority underlines the friendship between the USA and American Samoa, an unincorporated territory administered by the US Department of the Interior. The head of state is the US president, but the islands are ruled by an elected governor.

KIRIBATI

Republic of Kiribati

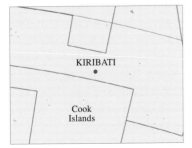

Flag proportions: 1:2
Adopted: 12 July 1979
Capital: Bairiki (on Tarawa)
Area: 717km² (277sq mi)
Population: 93,000
Language: Kiribati, English

Religion: Roman Catholic, Congregational
Currency: Australian dollar
Exports: Copra, coconuts, seaweed, re-exports, fish and fish products.

Kiribati's flag, an armorial banner, shows horizontal white and blue wavy lines, representing the Pacific Ocean. Rising from the sea is a gold radiant sun, above which flies a gold frigate bird symbolizing authority, freedom and command of the seas. Sun and bird are shown on a red field. The rising sun also stands for the equator. The arms date from 1937, and were created for the former British colony of the Gilbert and Ellice Islands. The shield was incorporated into the British Blue Ensign but, with independence in 1979, the islands became Kiribati and Tuvalu respectively. Kiribati opted for amended arms for its flag, while Tuvalu chose its own set of symbols.

FRENCH POLYNESIA

Territory of French Polynesia

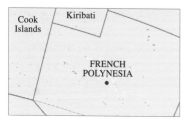

Flag proportions: 2:3
Adopted: 29 June 1985
Capital: Papeete
Area: 4,000km² (1,544sq mi)
Population: 246,000
Language: Tahitian, French
Religion: Evangelical Church of

Polynesia, Roman Catholic
Currency: French Pacific franc
Exports: Pearls, copra and other coconut products, mother-of-pearl, vanilla, fish (including shark meat).

French Polynesia is an overseas territory of France, so the *Tricolore* is its official flag, although a local flag featuring the Polynesian colours (red and white) is recognized. In a central circle is a *piragua* (a twin-hulled canoe), behind which is a gold sun. Blue and white denote the sea's wealth to be harvested, and piraguas are still used for fishing. Five rowers represent French Polynesia's *départéments*: Tuamotu Archipelago, Marquesas and Tubuai islands, and the Society Islands, comprising the Windward Islands or *Îles du Vent,* (Tahiti, Moorea, Maio, Tetiaroa, Mehetia) and the Leeward Islands or the *Îles sous le Vent,* (Raiatea, Huahine and Bora-Bora).

PITCAIRN ISLANDS

Pitcairn, Henderson, Ducie and Oeno Islands

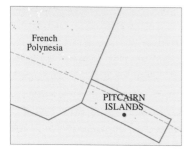

Flag proportions: 1:2
Adopted: 2 April 1984
Capital: Adamstown
Area: 47km² (18sq mi)
Population: 47

Languages: Pitkern, English
Religion: Seventh-Day Adventist
Currency: New Zealand dollar
Exports: Postage stamps, carvings, tourist goods.

The flag of this remote British overseas territory is the Blue Ensign with the Pitcairn Islands arms at the fly. The green triangle on the shield represents the islands rising from the sea. The anchor, representing security, and a depiction of the Bible are references to the HMS *Bounty*, as the Pitcairn community was founded after the famous mutiny in 1790. As a crest, a wooden Pitcairn wheelbarrow stands for vigour and industry. Also depicted is a branch of the miro plant. The territory, which includes Ducie and Oeno islands and the uninhabited coral atoll of Henderson Islands, falls under the British high commissioner in New Zealand.

NEW ZEALAND

New Zealand

Flag proportions: 1:2
Adopted: 12 June 1902
Capital: Wellington
Area: 270,534km²
(104,454sq mi)
Population: 4,028,000
Language: English, Maori

Religion: Non-religious, Anglican, Presbyterian, Roman Catholic
Currency: New Zealand dollar
Exports: Meat, dairy products, wood and wood products, fish, machinery, basic manufactured goods, minerals.

New Zealand's first flag, chosen by Maori chiefs in 1834, consisted of a red St George's cross, with another cross and four stars on a blue field in the chief canton. After the Treaty of Waitangi in 1840, in which the Maori ceded sovereignty to Britain in exchange for guaranteed possession of their land, the Union Flag became the official flag. The present flag originated in 1869 as a Blue Ensign for maritime use only, but became the national flag in 1902. The Union Flag is in the chief canton; the Southern Cross on the fly is made up of four white-bordered red stars with five points, no two stars being the same size.

TOKELAU

Tokelau

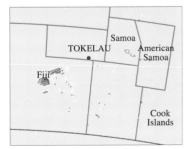

Flag proportions: 1:2
Adopted: n/a
Capital: There is no official capital: each of the three atolls has its own administration. There are three de facto capitals: Atafu, Fakaofo and Nukunonu
Area: 13 km2 (5 sq mi)

Population: 1,500
Language: Tokelauan, English
Religion: Congregational, Roman Catholic
Currency: New Zealand dollar
Exports: Postage stamps, copra, handicrafts.

Tokelau is a small dependency of New Zealand that comprises three atolls. The territory, which was settled by Polynesian migrants from neighbouring islands, became a British protectorate in 1889 but was transferred to New Zealand rule in 1925. The islands rejected self-government in referenda in 2006 and 2007. The territory flies the flag of New Zealand, but from the 1980s an unofficial blue flag, displaying three white stars and gold circles (for the three atolls) and a palm tree, began to be used for some international sports events. In 2006, a competition was held to select an official flag, dependent upon the atolls assuming self-government. This project was subsequently abandoned.

COOK ISLANDS

The Cook Islands

Flag proportions: 1:2
Adopted: 4 August 1979
Capital: Avarua
Area: 237 km² (92 sq mi)
Population: 19,600
Language: English, Cook Islands Maori

Religion: Cook Islands Christian Church, Roman Catholic
Currency: New Zealand dollar
Exports: Copra, fresh fruit (particularly papayas), tinned fruit, coffee, fish, clothing and footwear.

The Cook Islands, named for British explorer Captain James Cook, became a British possession in 1888 but their administration was transferred to New Zealand in 1900. In 1965, the islands became a self-governing state in free association with New Zealand, with complete internal autonomy and the right to declare independence at any time. However, economic dependence upon New Zealand has meant that the islands have maintained the status quo. The flag, the British ensign, symbolizes links with both Great Britain and New Zealand, while the circle of 15 white stars represent the 15 islands in the Cook Islands group.

NIUE

Niue

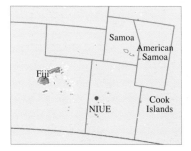

Flag proportions: 1:2
Adopted: 1975
Capital: Alofi
Area: 259 km² (100 sq mi)
Population: 1,600

Language: Niuean, English
Religion: Congregational, Mormon
Currency: New Zealand dollar
Exports: Coconut cream and copra, honey, fruit.

Niue is a small self-governing island in free association with New Zealand, with complete internal autonomy and the right to declare independence at any time. However, economic dependence upon New Zealand – the remote island relies upon aid from New Zealand, which is home to more than 20,000 Niueans – has encouraged Niue to maintain its present status rather than opt for sovereignty. Niue became a British protectorate in 1900, and was transferred to New Zealand the following year. Self-governing since 1974, Niue adopted a national flag in 1975. The flag is a variant on that of New Zealand, replacing the blue field with yellow (to symbolize the sun and friendship). The Southern Cross stars appear on the British Union flag in the canton, with an extra star added to represent Niue.

NORTH AMERICA, CENTRAL AMERICA AND THE CARIBBEAN

Originally only lightly populated by native Americans, the great northern continent was settled by Europeans (chiefly Spanish, French and British) from the mid-16th century. The same mix of explorers, seeking a westward route to India, encountered the Caribbean islands and the isthmus of Central America. To reach the Pacific, either an arduous overland journey was required, or a sea journey that involved negotiating the southern tip of South America, until the North-West Passage was opened up in 1904 and the Panama Canal began operations in 1914.

The heart of the region, in terms of both influence and population, is the United States. From the early 19th century, industrialization in Europe, as well as dynastic and social upheavals, led to a build-up of emigration to North America, principally to the USA. The North American Free Trade Agreement (NAFTA) was implemented in 1994. The participants in this system are the USA, Canada and Mexico. Prospective benefits include the creation of new jobs, higher wages in Mexico, ongoing environmental cleanups and improved health.

Colonization in the Caribbean depended on a plantation economy based on slave labour and, even after emancipation, on frank exploitation. Most slaves on the islands and in the southern states and territories of North America, were brought from West Africa, and their descendants and influence are still prominent today. While the islands explore alternative bases for their economies, most maintain economic links with the former colonial power.

Canada is slightly larger than the USA: 10 million km^2 to 9.6 million km^2. After Russia, it is the second largest country in the world. Mexico measures some 1.9 million km^2 and has a population of more than 103 million.

NORTH AMERICA AT A GLANCE

Largest country: Canada
Smallest country: St Kitts and Nevis
Largest city: Mexico City, Mexico
Major cities: Atlanta, Chicago, Dallas, Guadalajara, Guatemala City, Havana, Houston, Los Angeles, Monterey, Montréal, Nassau, New York, Ottawa, Philadelphia, Toronto, Vancouver

Highest point: Mt McKinley, Alaska, USA – 6,194m (20,320ft)
Lowest point: Death Valley, California, USA – 86m (282ft) below sea level)
Longest river: Mississippi-Missouri, USA – 6,020km (3,741mi)
Largest lake: Lake Superior, shared by Canada and USA – 82,350km^2 (31,800sq mi).

North America

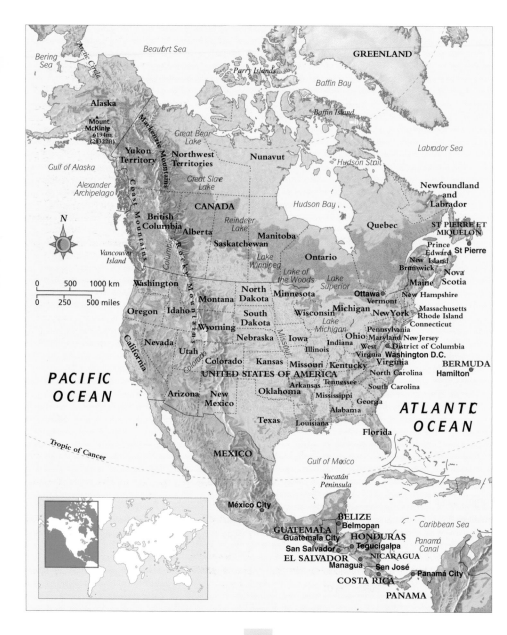

Bering Sea

Beaufort Sea

Arctic Circle

Parry Islands

GREENLAND

Baffin Bay

Alaska

Mount McKinley 6194m (20322ft)

Baffin Island

Mackenzie Mountains

Great Bear Lake

Yukon Territory

Northwest Territories

Nunavut

Labrador Sea

Gulf of Alaska

Hudson Strait

Alexander Archipelago

Coast Mountains

Great Slave Lake

Newfoundland and Labrador

N

British Columbia

CANADA

Reindeer Lake

Hudson Bay

Alberta

Manitoba

Quebec

ST PIERRE ET MIQUELON

Saskatchewan

Vancouver Island

Rocky Mountains

Columbia

Lake Winnipeg

Ontario

Prince Edward Island

St Pierre

New Brunswick

Nova Scotia

0   500   1000 km

0   250   500 miles

Washington

Montana

North Dakota

Lake of the Woods

Lake Superior

Ottawa

Maine

Vermont

New Hampshire

Oregon   Idaho

South Dakota

Minnesota

Wisconsin

Michigan

New York

Massachusetts

Rhode Island

Connecticut

Wyoming

Lake Michigan

Nebraska   Iowa

Ohio   Maryland New Jersey

Pennsylvania

Nevada

California

Missouri

Utah

Illinois

Indiana

West Virginia

District of Columbia

Washington D.C.

Colorado

Kansas

Missouri   Kentucky

Virginia

BERMUDA

Hamilton

PACIFIC OCEAN

UNITED STATES OF AMERICA

North Carolina

Arizona

New Mexico

Oklahoma

Arkansas

Tennessee

Mississippi

South Carolina

Georgia

ATLANTIC OCEAN

Texas

Alabama

Louisiana

Florida

Tropic of Cancer

MEXICO

Gulf of Mexico

Yucatán Peninsula

México City

BELIZE

Belmopan

Caribbean Sea

GUATEMALA

Guatemala City

HONDURAS

Panamá Canal

San Salvador

Tegucigalpa

EL SALVADOR

NICARAGUA

Managua

San José

Panamá City

COSTA RICA

PANAMA

Central America and the Caribbean

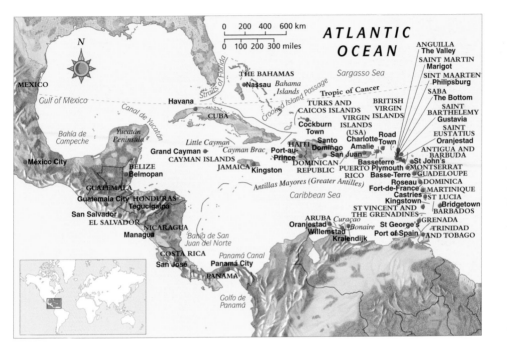

```
0    200   400   600 km
0   100  200  300 miles
```

ATLANTIC OCEAN

N

MEXICO

Gulf of México

Bahía de Campeche

Yucatán Peninsula

México City

THE BAHAMAS
Nassau *Bahama Islands*
Havana
CUBA
Little Cayman
Grand Cayman
Cayman Brac
CAYMAN ISLANDS
BELIZE
Belmopan
JAMAICA
Kingston

Straits of Florida

Crooked Island Passage

Tropic of Cancer

Sargasso Sea

TURKS AND CAICOS ISLANDS
Cockburn Town
HAITI
Port-au-Prince
Santo Domingo
DOMINICAN REPUBLIC
Antillas Mayores (Greater Antilles)

BRITISH VIRGIN ISLANDS
VIRGIN ISLANDS (USA)
San Juan
PUERTO RICO
Charlotte Amalie

ANGUILLA
The Valley
SAINT MARTIN
Marigot
SINT MAARTEN
Philipsburg
SABA
The Bottom
SAINT BARTHELEMY
Gustavia
SAINT EUSTATIUS
Oranjestad
Road Town
ANTIGUA AND BARBUDA
St John's
Basseterre
Basse-Terre
Plymouth
MONTSERRAT
GUADELOUPE
Roseau
DOMINICA
Fort-de-France
MARTINIQUE
Castries
ST LUCIA
Kingstown
ST VINCENT AND THE GRENADINES
Bridgetown
BARBADOS
GRENADA
St George's
TRINIDAD AND TOBAGO
Port of Spain

Caribbean Sea

GUATEMALA
Guatemala City
HONDURAS
Tegucigalpa
San Salvador
EL SALVADOR
NICARAGUA
Managua
Bahía de San Juan del Norte
COSTA RICA
San José
Panamá Canal
Panamá City
PANAMA

ARUBA
Oranjestad
Curaçao
Willemstad
Bonaire
Kralendijk

Golfo de Panamá

USA AT A GLANCE

Number of states: 50

Largest state: Alaska

Smallest state: Rhode Island

Capital: Washington DC (District of Columbia)

Ten largest US cities (in order of size): New York, Los Angeles, Chicago, Dallas, Philadelphia, Houston, Washington, Miami, Atlanta, Phoenix, Detroit.

Largest lake: Lake Superior – 82,100km² (31,699sq mi)

Longest river: Mississippi-Missouri 6,020km (3,741mi)

Highest point: Mt McKinley (Denali), Alaska – 6,194m (20,320ft); Mt Whitney, California – 4,418m (14,494ft) is the highest point in the lower 48 states

Lowest point: Death Valley, CA – 86m (282ft) below sea level.

NORTH AMERICA, CENTRAL AMERICA AND THE CARIBBEAN

UNITED STATES OF AMERICA

United States of America

Flag proportions: 10:19
Adopted: 4 July 1960
Capital: Washington DC
Area: 9,629,091km²
(3,717,796sq mi)
Population: 301,140,000
Language: English, Spanish

Religion: Roman Catholic, Baptist,
Methodist, Pentecostal
Currency: US dollar
Exports: Machinery and transport
equipment (particularly road
vehicles), industrial supplies and
raw materials, consumer goods.

The USA grew from 13 colonies that rose against the British government in April 1775. On New Year's Day, 1776, a flag was raised. Called the Continental Colours, it had the British Union Flag in the chief canton and 13 horizontal stripes. On 14 June, 1777, Congress adopted the first official flag, placing 13 white stars in the canton. In May 1795, when two more states joined the Union, two stars and stripes were added, making 15 of each. This version, known as the 'Star-Spangled Banner', was left unchanged until Congress passed the Flag Act of 1818, decreeing that while new stars might be added, the number of stripes was to revert to 13. The Stars and Stripes now has 50 stars, each depicting a state; and 13 stripes, for the original colonies. The last star was added in 1960, for Hawaii.

US STATE FLAGS

Date given is when the state joined the Union or ratified the Constitution.

Alabama	Alaska	Arizona	Arkansas	California
1819	1959	1912	1836	1850

Colorado	Connecticut	Delaware	District of Columbia	Florida
1876	1788	1787	(Federal Territory)	1845

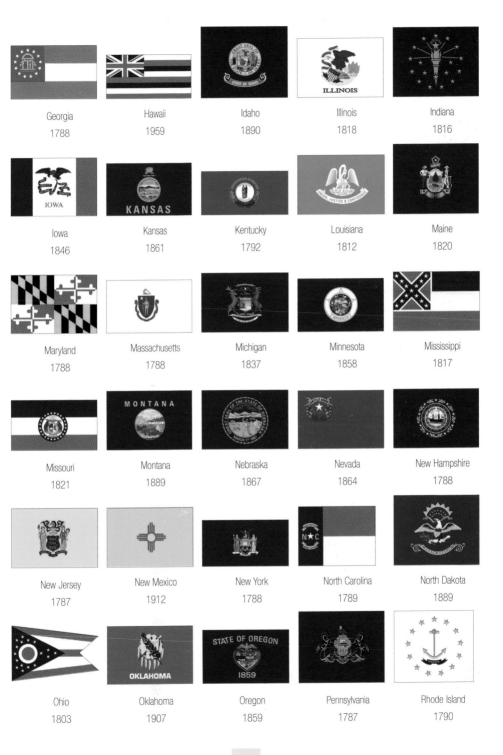

Georgia 1788	Hawaii 1959	Idaho 1890	Illinois 1818	Indiana 1816
Iowa 1846	Kansas 1861	Kentucky 1792	Louisiana 1812	Maine 1820
Maryland 1788	Massachusetts 1788	Michigan 1837	Minnesota 1858	Mississippi 1817
Missouri 1821	Montana 1889	Nebraska 1867	Nevada 1864	New Hampshire 1788
New Jersey 1787	New Mexico 1912	New York 1788	North Carolina 1789	North Dakota 1889
Ohio 1803	Oklahoma 1907	Oregon 1859	Pennsylvania 1787	Rhode Island 1790

US State Flags (continued)

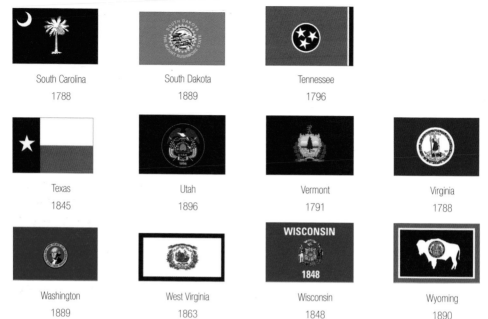

South Carolina	South Dakota	Tennessee
1788	1889	1796

Texas	Utah	Vermont	Virginia
1845	1896	1791	1788

Washington	West Virginia	Wisconsin	Wyoming
1889	1863	1848	1890

CANADA

Canada

CANADA   Hudson Bay

USA

Flag proportions: 1:2
Adopted: 15 February 1965
Capital: Ottawa
Area: 9,970,610km² (3,849,674 sq mi)
Population: 31,613,000
Languages: English, French
Religion: Roman Catholic, various Protestant churches
Currency: Canadian dollar
Exports: Motor vehicles, industrial, machinery, mineral fuels (petroleum and natural gas), aircraft, telecommunications equipment, chemicals, plastics, fertilizer, lumber, newsprint, pulp.

In 1867, Ontario, Nova Scotia, New Brunswick and Quebec united to form the Dominion of Canada, but it was to be almost 100 years before this country flew its own flag. During that time it used a version of the British Red Ensign. When designs for a national flag were called for in the 1960s, a popular version had a sprig of three red maple leaves between blue bands. The version eventually approved shows a single stylized red maple leaf on a white square, between two vertical bands of red. White represents the snow that covers much of the country in winter; red is for energy and in memory of the sacrifices made by Canadian servicemen and women in the two world wars.

GREENLAND

Greenland

Flag proportions: 2:3
Adopted: 6 June 1985
Capital: Nuuk
Area: 2,175,600km²
(839,800sq mi)
Population: 57,000
Languages: Greenland Inuit

(officially known as Inuktitut),
Danish
Religion: Evangelical Lutheran
Currency: Danish Krone
Exports: Fish and fish products.

Greenland was first inhabited by Eskimos from the North American Arctic. In about AD982, the Viking explorer, Eric the Red, established settlements on the west coast. A self-governing overseas territory of Denmark since 1979, the flag's colours are the same as those of the Danish flag. Greenlanders call their flag *Erfalasorput*, 'our flag', or *Aappalaaroq*, 'the red'. The large white part of the flag symbolizes an icecap, with the white half-circle being the icebergs and pack ice. Red stands for the ocean, with the fjords represented by the red half-circle. The circle also depicts the sun, which remains above the horizon during the brief summer months.

ST PIERRE ET MIQUELON

Saint Pierre and Miquelon

Flag proportions: 2:3
Adopted: c.1980
Capital: Saint Pierre
Area: 242km² (93sq mi)
Population: 6,300
Language: French

Religion: Roman Catholic
Currency: Euro
Exports: Fish and fish products,
shellfish, crustaceans, animal feed,
furs.

There are three islands in this French overseas territory. The last remnant of France's North American empire, it was settled in the 17th century by Basque and Breton fisherman. The unofficial flag is rich in heraldry. A high-prowed galleon under full sail recalls Jacques Cartier, who discovered the St Lawrence River in 1535. Blue depicts the Atlantic Ocean and the sky. The three emblems at the hoist commemorate the first colonists. In the chief canton, the Basque country is denoted by a green cross in saltire overlaid by a white cross, both on a red field. Brittany is represented by ermine, a fur, while Normandy is represented by two yellow lions.

BERMUDA

Bermuda

Flag proportions: 1:2
Adopted: October 1967
Capital: Hamilton
Area: 54km² (21sq mi)
Population: 62,100
Language: English

Religion: Anglican, Methodist, Roman Catholic
Currency: Bermuda dollar
Exports: Re-exported pharmaceuticals, fuel for shipping and aircraft.

Bermuda, a self-governing British overseas territory, consists of some 138 coral islands. An upmarket tourist destination and financial services centre, it enjoys one of the highest per capita incomes in the world. Many former British colonies fly a Blue or Red Ensign, usually 'defaced' with the Union Flag in the canton and the colony's badge at the fly. The Bermudan arms, granted in 1910, show a lion supporting a shield on which is displayed the wreck of the *Sea Venture*. The loss of this ship off Bermuda in 1609, and the subsequent dispatch of assistance from the mainland colony of Virginia, led to British colonization of the islands.

MEXICO

United States of Mexico

Flag proportions: 4:7
Adopted: 23 November 1968
Capital: México City
Area: 1,958,201km² (756,066sq mi)
Population: 103,264,000

Language: Spanish
Religion: Roman Catholic
Currency: Mexican peso
Exports: Manufactured goods, crude petroleum and oil products, silver, agricultural products.

The flag has three equal vertical bands of green, red and white (in the centre, with the coat of arms). Within a wreath, an eagle perched on a cactus plant, clasping a snake in its beak and claw, illustrates the Aztec legend of the founding of México City. When Mexico adopted its flag in 1821, green represented religion, white was for independence, and red for unity between the Spanish and the ethnic people. Since Liberal reform in 1860, green has stood for hope and natural resources; white for ethnicity, unity and purity; and red for the struggle for freedom and the blood of heroes.

GUATEMALA

The Republic of Guatemala

Flag proportions: 5:8
Adopted: 26 December 1997
Capital: Guatemala City
Area: 108,889km²
(42,042sq mi)
Population: 11,237,000
Language: Spanish, various

Mayan languages
Religion: Roman Catholic, various
Protestant Evangelical churches
Currency: Quetzal
Exports: Coffee, sugar, bananas,
vegetable seeds, beans,
cardamom, meat, clothing.

In 1823, following the overthrow of the Mexican Empire, Guatemala joined five former Spanish provinces in a short-lived political union known as the United Provinces of Central America, before becoming independent in 1823.

The flag is a vertical tricolour of light blue, for justice and steadfastness, and white for purity. The civil flag is plain, but the state flag depicts the national arms. Crossed swords and rifles with fixed bayonets represent justice and liberty. A scroll, inscribed '*Libertad 15 de Septiembre de 1821*', commemorates independence. A quetzal bird symbolizes the nation's liberty. Success and victory are represented by two branches of laurel.

HONDURAS

The Republic of Honduras

Flag proportions: 1:2
Adopted: 16 February 1866
Capital: According to the
constitution Tegucigalpa and
Comayagüela form the joint
capital
Area: 112,088km²
(43,277sq mi)

Population: 6,535,000
Language: Spanish
Religion: Roman Catholic,
Pentecostal
Currency: Lempira
Exports: Coffee, shrimp and
lobster, bananas, frozen meat,
zinc, timber.

Honduras was part of the great Mayan civilization whose city-states reached their zenith from about AD300–900, and endured until the Spanish conquest in the early 16th century. Discovered by Christopher Columbus, Honduras become a Spanish colony from 1526 until 1821, and was part of the United Provinces of Central America until 1838. The blue and white horizontal tribar derives from the United Provinces flag, with the five stars at the centre representing the former provinces. Blue represents sky and brotherhood, while white is for peace and purity.

EL SALVADOR

The Republic of El Salvador

Caribbean
Sea

Honduras

EL SALVADOR

Pacific
Ocean

Flag proportions: 4:7
Adopted: September 1972
Capital: San Salvador
Area: 21,041km² (8,124sq mi)
Population: 6,875,000
Language: Spanish

Religion: Roman Catholic,
Pentecostal
Currency: Colón and US dollar
Exports: Coffee, sugar, shrimps,
textiles, chemicals, beef, dairy
products.

El Salvador is the smallest country in Central America. The flag recalls the 1823 flag of the United Provinces of Central America. On a central white panel, behind a triangle representing the three branches of government (judicial, legislative and executive), are blue-and-white striped flags depicting the five provinces. Five volcanoes rise from the sea, and above their craters are a cap of liberty and a rainbow, the symbol of trust and hope. The arms are enclosed by a wreath tied in the national colours. The motto *Dios, Union, Libertad*, 'God, Unity and Freedom', is on a scroll beneath the triangle. The full name of the country encircles the arms.

NICARAGUA

The Republic of Nicaragua

Caribbean
Sea

Honduras

NICARAGUA

Pacific
Ocean

Flag proportions: 3:5
Adopted: 27 August 1971
Capital: Managua
Area: 130,670km²
(50,450sq mi)
Population: 5,142,000
Language: Spanish, Miskito

Religion: Roman Catholic,
Protestant Evangelical churches
Currency: Cordoba
Exports: Coffee, shrimps and
lobsters, cotton, tobacco,
bananas, meat, sugar.

Before the Spanish conquest, the Olmec, Maya and Aztec civilizations dominated Central America. The first European to reach Nicaragua, Gil Gonzalez de Avila, claimed the land for Spain in 1522. It remained under Spanish rule until 1821, then joined the United Provinces of Central America until independence in 1838, hence the blue-white-blue horizontal tribar of the flag. The arms are set within a triangle, the symbol of equality. Five volcanoes represent the members of the United Provinces, the sun and rainbow symbolize a bright future, and a cap of liberty stands for national freedom. Everything is encased within a circle made up of the name: Republica de Nicaragua, America Central.

COSTA RICA

The Republic of Costa Rica

Flag proportions: 3:5
Adopted: 5 May 1998
Capital: San José
Area: 51,100km² (19,730sq mi)
Population: 4,299,000
Language: Spanish
Religion: Roman Catholic, various

Protestant Evangelical churches
Currency: Costa Rica colón
Exports: Coffee, bananas, sugar, textiles, clothing, electronic equipment, medical equipment, flowers.

Costa Rica signed a Declaration of Independence from Spain in 1821, and was part of the United Provinces of Central America from 1823–38. The wife of the president is said to have designed the flag in 1848 to embody the ideals of the French Revolution: freedom, equality and brotherhood, and the colours of the *Tricolore*. The current flag has five horizontal stripes. The national arms are set within a white oval on the central red stripe, towards the hoist. Blue is for the sky, striving, intellectual thinking, perseverance and spiritual ideals. White is for happiness, wisdom and peace. Red is for the warmth, passion and generosity of the Costa Rican people, and their blood shed for freedom.

BELIZE

Belize

Flag proportions: 3:5
Adopted: 21 September 1981
Capital: Belmopan
Area: 22,965km² (8,867sq mi)
Population: 311,000
Language: English, English Creole, Spanish

Religion: Roman Catholic, Pentecostal, Anglican
Currency: Belize dollar
Exports: Sugar, bananas, citrus fruit, clothing, fish products, molasses, wood.

The Belize flag comprises a blue field with a red border at top and bottom. The colours are those of the leading political parties. At the centre of the blue panel, on a white disk, are the national arms, set within a circle of 50 leaves as a reminder that the People's United Party introduced the flag in 1950. The arms were granted in 1907 to British Honduras, as the country was formerly known. They retain some original features, depicting tools used in forestry and shipbuilding, and a mahogany tree for the logging industry. Two supporters, a Creole and a Mestizo, signify both diversity and joint effort. The motto, *Sub umbra floreo*, means 'I flourish in the shade'.

PANAMA

Republic of Panama

Flag proportions: 2:3
Adopted: 4 June 1904
Capital: Panama City (Ciudad de Panamá)
Area: 75,990km² (29,340sq mi)
Population: 3,228,000
Language: Spanish, English

Creole, Chibchan
Religion: Roman Catholic, Pentecostal
Currency: Balboa and US dollar
Exports: Bananas, shellfish, sugar, coffee, clothing.

When Panama's flag was created in 1903, it was baptized by Reverend Bernardino de la Concepción. Panama's political affiliations are represented on the flag by blue (Conservatives) and red (Liberals). White symbolizes the hope for peace through closer understanding between political adversaries.

Another explanation is that blue depicts the Pacific Ocean and the Caribbean, while red is for blood shed by Panamanian patriots. The five-pointed blue star stands for the civic virtue of honest administration and the red star for lawful authority.

BAHAMAS

The Commonwealth of the Bahamas

Flag proportions: 1:2
Adopted: 10 July 1973
Capital: Nassau
Area: 13,939km² (5,382sq mi)
Population: 304,000
Language: English, English Creole, French (Haitian) Creole

Religion: Baptist, Roman Catholic, Anglican
Currency: Bahamian dollar
Exports: Petroleum re-exports, fish, crayfish, rum, salt, chemicals.

The Bahamas was a British colony from 1783 to independence in 1973. Situated some 80km (50mi) southeast of Florida, it comprises 3,000 islands, only 22 of which are inhabited. The black triangle at the hoist represents the energy, force and determination of the population, while the equal horizontal bands of blue, gold, blue symbolize the country's warm seas and sunny beaches. A sunrise has been incorporated into the national arms.

Many merchant ships are registered in the Bahamas and fly the civil ensign – a red field quartered by a white cross, with the Bahamian flag in the chief canton.

TURKS AND CAICOS

Turks and Caicos Islands

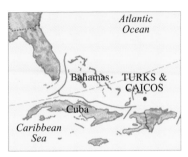

Flag proportions: 1:2
Adopted: 7 November 1968
Capital: Cockburn Town
Area: 430km² (166sq mi)
Population: 33,200

Language: English
Religion: Baptist, Anglican,
Methodist
Currency: US dollar
Exports: Lobster, conch, fish.

This archipelago of 40 islands (eight inhabited), which lies southeast of the Bahamas, is a British overseas territory. Most smaller overseas territories (formerly crown colonies) use the British Blue Ensign, with the colony's arms or shield depicted at the fly. Some older ensigns show the arms on a white disc, but the arms are now mostly placed directly against the blue field. The arms of Turks and Caicos show a yellow shield with a queen conch shell, once widely used for currency; a spiny lobster, the basis of a major industry; and a Turk's Head cactus, a plant unique to the islands.

CUBA

The Republic of Cuba

Flag proportions: 1:2
Adopted: 20 May 1902
Capital: Havana (La Habana)
Area: 110,861km²
(42,804sq mi)
Population: 11,239,000
Language: Spanish

Religion: Non-religious, Roman
Catholic
Currency: Cuban peso
Exports: Sugar, minerals,
tobacco, fish products, medical
products.

In 1849 a group of Cuban exiles approved a proposal from Miguel Teurbe Tolón for a flag to be used in the attempt to liberate their island from Spanish rule. Tolón's design, inspired by the US Stars and Stripes, eventually became the national flag of Cuba. In an official description, the blue bars represent the three former provinces of the island; white is testimony to the purity of the ideal of independence; the triangle signifies liberty, equality and fraternity; and the star symbolizes freedom and independence, attained by spilling the blood of patriots, whose sacrifices are recalled by the red triangle.

JAMAICA

Jamaica

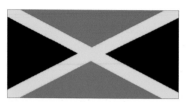

Flag proportions: 1:2
Adopted: 6 August 1962
Capital: Kingston
Area: 10,991km² (4,244sq mi)
Population: 2,608,000
Language: English, English Creole

Religion: Church of God, Baptist, Seventh-day Adventist, Pentecostal
Currency: Jamaican dollar
Exports: Alumina, bauxite, sugar, bananas, rum, chemicals, clothing.

Yellow stands for sunshine and natural resources, black for the burdens borne by the people, and green for agriculture and hope for the future. An unofficial motto is: 'Hardships there are, but the land is green and the sun still shineth'. Black, green and gold are Pan-African colours, and most Jamaicans are descended from black people who were brought from Africa as slaves.

CAYMAN ISLANDS

Cayman Islands

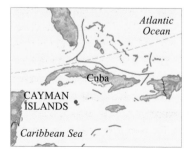

Flag proportions: 1:2
Adopted: 24 November 1988
Capital: George Town
Area: 259km² (100sq mi)
Population: 39,400

Language: English
Religion: United Church, Anglican
Currency: Cayman Islands dollar
Exports: Turtle products, manufactured consumer goods.

The low-lying Grand Cayman, Cayman Brac and Little Cayman islands were a pirate lair from the 17th century. Colonized by Britain, the Caymans were a dependency of Jamaica until they became a crown colony (now an overseas territory) in 1962. The flag is the Blue Ensign with the Cayman arms, granted in 1958, on the fly. Three stars represent the islands; the lion signifies the link with Britain; a turtle and a pineapple represent the local fauna and flora; and blue and white wavy bars depict the sea. A scroll bears the motto 'He hath founded it upon the seas', in tribute to the islands' origins.

PUERTO RICO

The Commonwealth of Puerto Rico

Flag proportions: 2:3
Adopted: 24 July 1952
Capital: San Juan
Area: 8,897km² (3,435sq mi)
Population: 3,912,000
Language: Spanish, English
Religion: Roman Catholic

Currency: US dollar
Exports: Pharmaceuticals, chemicals and chemical products, electronics, clothing, food (particularly canned tuna, rum and beverages), medical equipment.

Claimed by Spain in 1493 after Columbus's second voyage to the Americas, the island became a colonial possession for 400 years, during which the indigenous population was nearly exterminated, and African slave labour introduced. The 1898 Spanish-American war resulted in the cession of Puerto Rico to the USA. Puerto Ricans were granted US citizenship in 1917, and have repeatedly chosen to retain their commonwealth status.

Puerto Rico's flag resembles that of Cuba, with the colours reversed, as both were originally designed as anti-Spanish, pro-US emblems. The star depicts the country, and the triangle proclaims liberty, equality and fraternity.

HAITI

The Republic of Haiti

Flag proportions: 3:5
Adopted: 25 February 1986
Capital: Port-au-Prince
Area: 27,750km² (10,714sq mi)
Population: 7,929,000
Language: French, French-Haitian Creole

Religion: Roman Catholic, Baptist, Voodoo
Currency: Gourde
Exports: Textiles and clothing, electrical goods, handicrafts, coffee, vegetable oils, cocoa.

A former French colony, Haiti proclaimed independence in 1804, following a rebellion the previous year. Haitian leaders in the struggle created a blue and red flag on 18 May 1803. The two stripes symbolized the black and mixed-race peoples of the country. In 1840 the stripes were made horizontal and the coat of arms placed at the centre. Haiti's arms include cannons and cannon balls, trumpets, a drum, and muskets with fixed bayonets, backed by six Haitian flags. A palm surmounted by a cap of liberty symbolizes independence. The weapons indicate a willingness to fight for freedom. The motto, *L'Union Fait La Force*, means 'Union Makes Strength.'

DOMINICAN REPUBLIC

The Dominican Republic

Flag proportions: 5:8
Adopted: 21 August 1943
Capital: Santo Domingo
Area: 48,443km² (18,704sq mi)
Population: 8,562,000
Language: Spanish

Religion: Roman Catholic, various Protestant Evangelical churches
Currency: Dominican peso
Exports: Ferronickel, raw sugar, gold, silver, coffee, cocoa, tobacco, meat, consumer goods.

In 1844, the Trinitarians, who were fighting to liberate their country from Haitian rule, changed the Haitian flag by quartering it with a white cross, to signify the Catholic faith, and altering the colours so the first and fourth quarters are blue, and the second and third quarters red. This is the civil flag, as flown by citizens on land and at sea, but for national and state use the coat of arms is placed at the centre of the cross. A shield, of the same pattern as the flag, is behind a trophy of Dominican flags supporting a crucifix and a Bible, open at St John's Gospel. Blue stands for liberty, red for the fire and blood of the independence struggle. The white cross is a symbol of sacrifice.

VIRGIN ISLANDS

Virgin Islands of the United States

Flag proportions: 2:3 or 3:5
Adopted: 17 May 1921
Capital: Charlotte Amalie
Area: 352km² (136sq mi)
Population: 110,000

Language: English, Spanish
Religion: Baptist, Roman Catholic
Currency: US dollar
Exports: Refined petroleum.

St Thomas, St Croix and St John, plus about 50 small islets, form an unincorporated territory of the USA, with residents electing a governor and legislature. From the 18th century, the Virgin Islands were owned by England and Denmark, but the USA purchased the Danish portion in 1917.

The emblem is partly derived from the US arms. It consists of a bald eagle on a white field, displayed *affronté* (showing its front), with its head turned to the side and wings and legs spread. In its right talon it clasps a laurel branch, and in its left talon three arrows represent the main islands. On its front is a shield with a blue chief and seven white and six red vertical stripes. The initials V and I, on either side of the eagle, stand for Virgin Islands.

BRITISH VIRGIN ISLANDS

British Virgin Islands

Flag proportions: 1:2
Adopted: 15 November 1960
Capital: Road Town
Area: 153km² (59sq mi)
Population: 21,000
Language: English

Religion: Methodist, Anglican, Roman Catholic
Currency: US dollar
Exports: Rum, fresh fish, fruit, gravel, sand.

The Virgin Islands were discovered by Columbus in 1494. As they seemed innumerable, he named them after the followers of St Ursula who, along with 11,000 virgin companions, was martyred during the Dark Ages. Settled by the Dutch in 1648, the islands were annexed by Britain in 1672. A self-governing overseas territory of the UK, the British Virgin Islands (BVI) comprise Tortola, Virgin Gorda, Anegada, Jost van Dykes and about 40 islets. The economy is linked to the US Virgin Islands. Set on the Blue Ensign, the BVI's badge, which dates from 1960, shows St Ursula holding a lamp. The 11 lamps symbolize her followers. The scroll's Latin motto reads *Vigilate* (be watchful).

ANGUILLA

Anguilla

Flag proportions: 1:2
Adopted: 30 May 1990
Capital: The Valley
Area: 96km² (37sq mi)
Population: 11,600

Language: English, Creole
Religion: Anglican, Methodist
Currency: East Caribbean dollar
Exports: Lobster, fish, livestock, salt.

A British colony from 1650, Anguilla declared itself a republic in 1967, following a dispute against incorporation with St Christopher-Nevis. Since 1980, it has been a dependency (now an overseas territory) of the UK. The flag's design originated with a former Governor of Anguilla. When a British Red or Blue Ensign carries a depiction of a badge or coat of arms at the fly, the ensign is said to be 'defaced'. Anguilla's flag is the Blue Ensign defaced with a shield on which three dolphins leap on a white field (their interlocking circular design represents unity and strength) above a wavy turquoise base, symbolizing the Caribbean Sea.

ST KITTS AND NEVIS

The Federation of Saint Kitts and Nevis

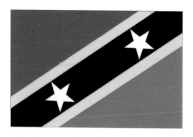

Caribbean Sea

Flag proportions: 2:3
Adopted: 19 September 1983
Capital: Basseterre
Area: 269km² (101sq mi)
Population: 46,000
Language: English, English Creole

Religion: Anglican, Methodist, Moravian
Currency: East Caribbean dollar
Exports: Electronic goods, machinery, sugar, beverages, tobacco.

Named by Columbus in 1493, St Christopher (St Kitts) became Britain's first West Indian colony in 1623; Nevis was settled soon afterwards. Part of the Leeward Islands' Federation from 1871–1956, the islands formed a colony with the British Virgin Islands until 1960, were granted self-government in 1967, and gained independence within the Commonwealth in September 1983. The flag uses Pan-African colours, with green for the land's fertility, red for the struggle from slavery through colonialism to independence, yellow for year-round sunshine and black for the people's African heritage. Two white stars on the black diagonal band are said to represent the islands, but actually express hope and freedom.

ANTIGUA AND BARBUDA

Antigua and Barbuda

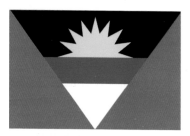

Caribbean Sea

Flag proportions: 2:3
Adopted: 27 February 1967
Capital: St John's
Area: 442km² (171sq mi)
Population: 76,900
Language: English, English Creole

Religion: Anglican, Moravian, Roman Catholic
Currency: East Caribbean dollar
Industries: Re-exported petroleum products, manufactured goods, food products (fruit and alcohol).

Antigua and Barbuda were British colonies from 1632 until independence in 1981. When the colony received self-government in 1967, a new flag was designed by local citizen Reginald Samuel, who described it as depicting a sun of hope rising in a new era, set against the background of the people's African heritage. The letter 'V' formed by the red triangles foretells victory, and red symbolizes the energy of the people. Blue represents the all-surrounding sea and white is for hope.

MONTSERRAT

Montserrat

Flag proportions: 1:2
Adopted: 1960, revised 1999
Capital: Brades (de facto)
Area: 98km² (38sq mi)
Population: 9,000
Language: English

Religion: Anglican, Methodist, Pentecostal
Currency: East Caribbean dollar
Exports: Electronic components, plastic bags, peppers and other foodstuffs, cattle.

Montserrat was named by Columbus in 1493 for an eponymous mountain in northeast Spain (*monte serrado*, jagged mountain). It became a British crown colony in 1871, and is now an overseas territory. The Blue Ensign is set with the island's badge at the fly. Comprising a shield on a white disc, it depicts a woman in an ankle-length garment, standing on a reddish-brown base beneath a blue sky. Recalling the arrival of Irish immigrants in 1632, she holds a cross in her right hand and a harp in her left.

In July 1995, the Soufriere Hills volcano began erupting, resulting in wide-spread devastation. Major volcanic activity in 1997 forced the closure of air and seaports and the evacuation of many islanders.

GUADELOUPE

The département of Guadeloupe

Flag proportions: 2:3
Adopted: n/a
Capital: Basse-Terre
Area: 1,628km² (629sq mi)
Population: 386,000

Language: French, French Creole
Religion: Roman Catholic
Currency: Euro
Exports: Bananas, sugar, rum, melons.

A French possession since 1635, the Guadeloupe archipelago consists of seven inhabited islands, the two largest being Basse-Terre and Grande-Terre. All French overseas departments fly the *Tricolore* as the official flag, however, a flag representing the department is permitted to be flown alongside the *Tricolore*. Guadeloupe's flag is horizontally divided, with the lower portion showing a radiant yellow sun and a green sheaf of sugar cane on a black or red field. The upper portion, which is one third of the flag's depth, has three yellow *fleurs de lis* on a blue field.

SAINT MARTIN

Saint-Martin

Flag proportions: 2:3
Adopted: n/a
Capital: Marigot
Area: 54km² (21sq mi)
Population: 29,100

Language: French, English
Creole
Religion: Roman Catholic
Currency: Euro
Exports: Re-exported goods, fish.

The Caribbean island of Saint Martin is the smallest landmass divided between two countries: since 1648, the northern part of the island has been a French possession, while the southern part, Sint Maarten, has belonged to the Netherlands (see page 133). Annexed to the French overseas département (province) of Guadeloupe, Saint-Martin had more in common with its Dutch neighbour – with which it has shared free port status since 1936 – than with distant Guadeloupe. Consequently, when a referendum was held in Saint-Martin in 2003, the territory's voters opted for separation. In July 2007, Saint-Martin became a separate French dependency (a collectivity) and has continued to fly the French flag.

SAINT-BARTHELEMY

Saint-Barthélemy

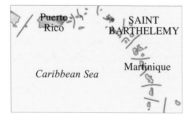

Flag proportions: 1:2
Adopted: 1998
Capital: Gustavia
Area: 21km² (8sq mi)
Population: 6,800

Language: French
Religion: Roman Catholic
Currency: Euro
Exports: Bananas, melon, salt, livestock.

The tiny island of Saint-Barthélemy became French in 1665, but, in 1784, France sold it to Sweden. Unlike other Caribbean islands, it did not import slaves from Africa in early colonial times; consequently, the population is largely European. Saint-Barthélemy became prosperous as a free port and, in 1878, Sweden sold the island back to France. In a referendum in 2003, Saint-Barthélemy opted for separation from the French island of Guadeloupe (to which it was administratively attached) and, in July 2007, the island became a separate French dependency, a collectivity. It flies the French flag but also has its own local flag, which displays Saint-Barthélemy's arms on a white field.

DOMINICA

Commonwealth of Dominica

Flag proportions: 1:2
Adopted: 3 November 1990
Capital: Roseau
Area: 739km² (285sq mi)
Population: 71,000

Language: English, French Creole
Religion: Roman Catholic
Currency: East Caribbean dollar
Exports: Bananas, soap, bay oil, vegetables, grapefruit.

A former French colony, Dominica was ceded to Britain in 1763, became a colony in 1805 and gained independence in 1978. The flag has a green field divided into four by a centred cross of equal stripes of yellow, black and white. Ten green five-pointed stars within a red disc represent Dominica's parishes, or administrative divisions. At the centre of the disc, a sisserou parrot (*Psittacus imperialis*) symbolizes flight and the attainment of greater heights in fulfilling ambitions. Green depicts the lush vegetation of the land. The tricoloured cross represents the Trinity; its colours are yellow for the Carib people and the sunshine, black for the dark, fertile soil and the island's African heritage, and white for rivers and the purity of hope.

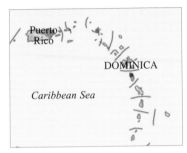

MARTINIQUE

The département of Martinique

Flag proportions: 2:3
Adopted: 4 August 1766
Capital: Fort-de-France
Area: 1,128km² (436sq mi)
Population: 381,000

Language: French, Creole
Religion: Roman Catholic
Currency: Euro
Exports: Refined petroleum, bananas, rum, pineapples.

Discovered by Spanish explorers in 1493, the island of Martinique became a French colony in 1635. It has been an overseas territory of France since 1972. As such, the official flag is the *Tricolore*, but local use is made of a blue flag quartered with a white cross that was flown by French ships prior to the 1789 Revolution. The flag was rediscovered around 1935 and has since become a local symbol. In each quarter is a rearing snake extending its forked tongue, all in white. The snake's body resembles the capital letter 'L', as the flag was that of the former French colony of St Lucia and Martinique and was flown by French merchant ships based on the two islands.

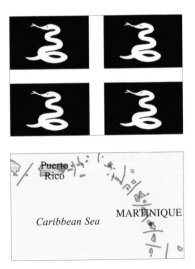

SAINT LUCIA

Saint Lucia

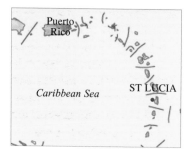

Flag proportions: 1:2
Adopted: 27 February 1979
Capital: Castries
Area: 617km² (238sq mi)
Population: 158,000
Language: English,

French Creole
Religion: Roman Catholic
Currency: East Caribbean dollar
Exports: Bananas, other
foodstuffs (coconut oil, cocoa,
fruit, vegetables), clothing.

First settled in 1605, St Lucia was the subject of dispute between Britain and France until 1814, when it was ceded to Britain. It gained independence in 1979. Against a blue field, representing the Atlantic Ocean, a yellow triangle overlies the base of a black isosceles triangle outlined in white. The triangles depict two local volcanic peaks, the Pitons. Yellow is for sunshine, while black and white symbolize the island's dual African and European cultural heritage.

BARBADOS

Barbados

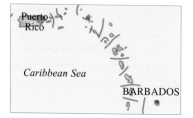

Flag proportions: 2:3
Adopted: 30 November 1966
Capital: Bridgetown
Area: 430km² (166sq mi)
Population: 272,000
Language: English, Bajan/English
Creole

Religion: Anglican, Pentecostal,
Methodist
Currency: Barbados dollar
Exports: Sugar, molasses, rum,
chemicals, electrical components,
margerine, clothing.

From 1627, British settlement in Barbados was based on a sugar-plantation economy. The former crown colony achieved self-government in 1961 and independence in 1966. Vertical bands of blue and golden yellow evoke the shores of Barbados washed by the Atlantic Ocean. The central band bears a trident, which symbolizes control over the sea. The trident lacks its shaft, indicating the break with the past that came with independence. (The former colonial badge and seal depicted the seated figure of Britannia with a shield and trident.)

SAINT VINCENT AND THE GRENADINES

Saint Vincent and the Grenadines

Caribbean Sea

ST VINCENT & THE GRENADINES

Flag proportions: 2:3
Adopted: 22 October 1985
Capital: Kingstown
Area: 389km² (150sq mi)
Population: 103,000
Language: English,

English Creole
Religion: Anglican, Methodist,
Pentecostal
Currency: East Caribbean dollar
Exports: Bananas, taro, arrowroot
starch, tennis racquets.

Occupied by Britain from 1762, St Vincent and the Grenadines achieved independence in 1979. The flag has a broad yellow vertical band between narrower bands of blue (at the hoist) and green. In the central band, three green diamonds form a 'V' for St Vincent. The diamonds and flag are popularly known as 'the Gems', from the islands' slogan, the 'Gems of the Antilles'. An official description states: 'The diamonds reflect the plural nature of the many islands. Blue represents the sky and sea. Gold is for warmth, the bright spirit of the people and the golden sands of the Grenadines. Green represents the lush vegetation and the enduring vitality of the people.'

GRENADA

Grenada

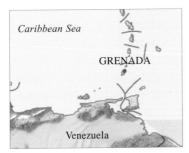

Caribbean Sea

GRENADA

Venezuela

Flag proportions: 1:2
Adopted: 7 February 1974
Capital: Saint George's
Area: 344km² (133sq mi)
Population: 103,000
Language: English, English Creole

Religion: Roman Catholic,
Anglican
Currency: East Caribbean dollar
Exports: Bananas, cocoa,
nutmeg, citrus fruit, clothing,
mace.

Grenada was discovered by Columbus in 1498 and settled by France in 1650. A British colony from 1783, it achieved self-government in 1967 and independence in 1974. Sometimes called the 'Spice Island', Grenada carries a depiction of a nutmeg on its flag as it is the world's second largest supplier of this pungent spice. The red border symbolizes courage and harmony, yellow is for the sun and for friendliness, and green for the natural vegetation and agriculture. Stars represent the parishes of Grenada, with the central star, on a red disc, depicting the capital, St George's.

TRINIDAD AND TOBAGO

Republic of Trinidad and Tobago

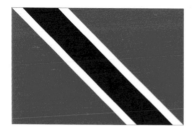

Caribbean Sea

TRINIDAD & TOBAGO

Venezuela

Flag proportions: 2:3
Adopted: 31 August 1962
Capital: Port of Spain
Area: 5,128km² (1,980sq mi)
Population: 1,262,000
Language: English, Trinidad English Creole

Religion: Roman Catholic, Hindu, Anglican, Sunni Islam
Currency: Trinidad and Tobago dollar
Exports: Refined petroleum, crude petroleum and petroleum products, chemicals, iron, steel, fertilizer.

Trinidad and Tobago were visited by Columbus in 1498 and colonized by Spain in 1532. Trinidad was ceded to Britain in 1802 and Tobago in 1814. Separate until 1889, they achieved independence within the Commonwealth in 1962, becoming a republic in 1976. Red represents the vitality of the land and people, the sun's warmth and energy, and courage and friendliness. White is for the sea, the cradle of heritage, the purity of aspirations and the equality of men. Black represents the people's dedication as well as the land's strength, unity, purpose and wealth. The colours represent the republic's past, present and future and serve as inspiration for a united, vital, free and dedicated people.

CURACAO

Curaçao

CURACAO

Caribbean Sea

Venezuela

Flag proportions: 2:3
Adopted: 1984
Capital: Willemstad
Area: 444km² (171sq mi)
Population: 136,000
Language: Dutch, Papiamento

Religion: Roman Catholic
Currency: Curaçao florin
Exports: Refined petroleum, re-exported crude petroleum, consumer goods.

Curaçao has been Dutch almost continuously since 1634. The island, off the coast of Venezuela, became the administrative seat of the Netherlands Antilles, which in 1954 became a self-governing Dutch territory. The different islands in the federation had different needs and aspirations, and Curaçao, larger and more prosperous than the other islands, opted for separation in a plebiscite in 2005, becoming a separate self-governing state in association with the Netherlands in 2008. The island's flag is blue, symbolizing the sea, with a gold bar, symbolizing the sun. The two stars represent the islands of Curaçao and Klein Curaçao.

BONAIRE

Kingdom's Island of Bonaire

Flag proportions: 1:2
Adopted: 1996
Capital: Kralendijk
Area: 288km² (111sq mi)
Population: 10,600
Language: Dutch, Papiamento,
Spanish
Religion: Roman Catholic, Dutch Reformed
Currency: Euro
Exports: Re-exported crude petroleum, salt, aloes, textiles.

The small, dry island of Bonaire, east of the larger Dutch island of Curaçao, became Dutch in 1633 and became part of the Netherlands Antilles in 1845. Following a referendum in 2005, the self-governing Netherlands Antilles federation was abolished, and, in 2008, Bonaire became an overseas territory of the Netherlands, with limited local government. The island's flag has two triangles separated by a white stripe: the blue triangle represents the sea, while the smaller yellow triangle symbolizes the island's flowers. A stylized black compass, representing navigation, is seen in the white stripe.

SINT MAARTEN

Sint Maarten

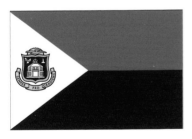

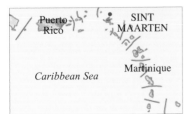

Flag proportions: 1:2
Adopted: 1985
Capital: Philipsburg
Area: 34km² (13sq mi)
Population: 35,000
Language: Dutch, English
Religion: Dutch Reformed
Currency: Florin
Exports: Financial services, consumer goods.

Sint-Maarten is the Dutch half of the island of Saint Martin, which, in 1648, was divided between France and the Netherlands. Part of the Netherlands Antilles since 1845, Sint Maarten shared free port status with Saint-Martin (the French part of the island) from 1936, and both territories became prosperous. In 2008, the Netherlands Antilles federation was abolished, and Sint Maarten became an internally self-governing state in association with the Netherlands. The territory's flag is red, white, and blue, reflecting the Dutch national colours. The flag has a badge displaying symbols of Sint Maarten, including the national bird (the pelican), the courthouse in the capital, and the monument marking the border between Sint Maarten and Saint-Martin.

SABA

Kingdom's Island of Saba	

Flag proportions: 2:3
Adopted: 1 January 1986
Capital: The Bottom
Area: 13km² (5sq mi)
Population: 1,430

Language: English, Dutch
Religion: Roman Catholic
Currency: Euro
Exports: Potatoes, consumer goods.

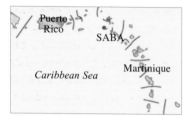

Dutch since 1630, the tiny island of Saba, which is an extinct volcano, is largely English speaking. Saba became part of the Netherlands Antilles in 1845, but when that self-governing federation was abolished in 2008, the voters of Saba opted for the status of a separate overseas territory of the Netherlands, with limited local government. The island, which has poor soil, is economically dependent upon the Dutch government. Saba's flag contains a central white diamond (said to represent peace), on which is a gold star, which represents the island. The lower blue triangles are said to represent the sea, while the upper red triangles are variously said to symbolize courage or unity.

SAINT EUSTATIUS

Kingdom's Island of Saint Eustatius	

Flag proportions: 1:2
Adopted: 2004
Capital: Oranjestad
Area: 21km² (8sq mi)
Population: 2,600

Language: English, Dutch
Religion: Roman Catholic
Currency: Euro
Exports: Lobsters, vegetables.

The largely English-speaking Dutch island of Saint Eustatius, popularly known as Statia, comprises two extinct volcanoes. These peaks appear in green in profile at the centre of a white diamond on the territory's flag. Statia has been Dutch for most of the period since 1636, and became known as the Golden Rock for the prosperity it gained from the slave trade in the eighteenth century. Like the other Dutch islands in the Caribbean, Statia became part of the Netherlands Antilles in 1845 and, when the Netherlands Antilles federation was dissolved in 2008, the island became a separate overseas territory of the Netherlands, with limited local government.

ARUBA

Aruba

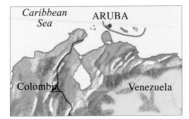

Flag proportions: 2:3
Adopted: 1 January 1986
Capital: Oranjestad
Area: 193km² (75sq mi)
Population: 91,000
Language: Dutch, Papiamento

Religion: Roman Catholic
Currency: Aruban florin
Exports: Refined petroleum, food and live animals, art and collectibles, machinery, electrical equipment, fish.

Discovered by Spain in 1499, Aruba was claimed by the Dutch in 1636. It seceded from the Netherlands Antilles in 1986 to become an autonomous member of the Kingdom of the Netherlands. On a field of United Nations' blue are two yellow stripes close to the lower edge of the flag, with a red four-pointed star, outlined in white, in the chief canton. Blue depicts the sky and the Caribbean Sea, the star represents the main languages of Aruba and the four corners of the earth from which its people have come to settle. The star is also Aruba itself, with its red soils fringed with white beaches. The yellow stripes symbolize the indigenous rain-flower, as well as the sun, tourism and mineral resources that are the mainstay of Aruba's economy.

 # SOUTH AMERICA

South America extends from the Caribbean Sea to the Strait of Magellan and Cape Horn. The total area amounts to 17.8 million km² (6.8 million sq mi). The continent's states are sometimes referred to as Latin America, from its Spanish and Portuguese language origins. A few northerly states, though, inherited the French, English and Dutch languages. Many South Americans are a blend of Spanish, Portuguese, indigenous Indians and African slaves.

Portuguese-speaking Brazil, with a population of nearly 184 million, represents about half the people and the land of South America. For several decades in the 19th century, Brazil was an empire. The great ancient civilization, the Incas, had its homeland in the Andes Mountains of Peru.

Many South American countries are well endowed with minerals, oil and natural gas. Agricultural products include coffee, cocoa, meat, fruit, wool and cotton. In the north, the trade in illegal drugs, such as cocaine, continues to earn a significant amount of foreign currency.

Geographically, South America is dominated by the Andes, extending north to south for some 7,250km (4,500mi). Mighty rivers, such as the Amazon and Orinoco, flow eastward through the extensive equatorial rainforests, which are falling prey to slash-and-burn farming and over-exploitation. South of the forest zone are the wide, temperate plains of Argentina – cattle country supreme. To the west, a coastal plain of largely arid desert stretches from Peru to Chile.

The Falkland Islands form part of the continent. Here, the prospect of offshore oilfields led to conflict in 1982 between rival claimants Argentina and Great Britain. Britain retains possession of the islands, called the Malvinas by Argentina, and of unpromising territory further south towards Antarctica.

AT A GLANCE

Biggest country: Brazil
Smallest country: Suriname
Biggest city: São Paolo, Brazil
Major cities: Belo Horizonte, Bogotá, Buenos Aires, Caracas, Lima, Pôrto Alegre, Rio de Janeiro, Santiago
Highest point: Aconcagua, Argentina – 6,960m

(22,834ft) – the highest peak in the western hemisphere
Lowest point: Valdés Peninsula, Argentina (40m (131ft) below sea level)
Longest river: Amazon 6,448km (4,007mi)
Largest lake: Titicaca, Bolivia/Peru 8340km² (3,220 sq mi).

South America

Freedom from colonization

Much of South America was colonized by Spain and Portugal in the early 16th century, but by 1800 there was strong agitation for independence. Among the earliest revolutionary leaders was Francisco de Miranda, a Venezuelan who, in 1806, raised a flag that consisted of equal horizontal bands of yellow above blue above red. Blue represents the Atlantic Ocean, separating the New World (yellow) from Spanish tyranny (red).

Venezuela, Ecuador and Colombia all adopted versions of de Miranda's flag. Venezuela's flag has the same colours and divisions, plus an arc of seven small stars in the blue band.

Different emblems of freedom are depicted on many South American flags. The flags of Argentina and Uruguay feature a prominent golden radiant sun with the orb depicting a human face. On the Argentinian flag the sun commemorates the first mass demonstration in favour of independence (25 May 1810), when a bright sun broke through cloudy skies. This national symbol of Argentina represents liberty or freedom. A sun also appears on the flags of Bolivia and Ecuador.

A cap of liberty is depicted on the flag of Paraguay and the flag or coat of arms of several other South American countries. In heraldry, it is always red.

FLAGS BASED ON DE MIRANDA'S FLAG

Venezuela

Ecuador

Colombia

ECUADOR

Republic of Ecuador

Flag proportions: 1:2
Adopted: 7 November 1900
Capital: Quito
Area: 269,178km² (103,930sq mi)
Population: 12,157,000
Language: Spanish, Quechua
Religion: Roman Catholic

Currency: US dollar
Exports: Crude petroleum and petroleum products, food and food products (particularly bananas, shrimp, coffee, cocoa and fish), cut flowers.

An Inca kingdom before the Spanish conquest in the 16th century, Ecuador joined Gran Colombia in 1822, seceding from the federation in 1830 to form a republic. The flag is similar to Colombia and Venezuela's flags, but with the national arms at the centre. These incorporate a ship at the mouth of the Guayas River, representing trade and commerce; a sun of liberty; an axe and bundles of rods as symbols of republicanism; four signs of the Zodiac, recalling the 1845 revolution; and the snow-capped Mt Chimborazo, surmounted by an Andean condor, signifying courage and freedom.

COLOMBIA

The Republic of Colombia

Flag proportions: 2:3
Adopted: 26 November 1861
Capital: Bogotá
Area: 1,141,568km² (440,762sq mi)
Population: 43,942,000
Language: Spanish

Religion: Roman Catholic
Currency: Colombian peso
Exports: Petroleum products, coffee, coal, textiles and clothing, bananas, cut flowers, forestry products.

A Spanish possession from the 16th century, Colombia was liberated in 1819 by Simón Bolívar, a South American revolutionary leader. In 1822, Ecuador, Colombia and Venezuela formed the republic of Gran Colombia. Colombia became a separate republic in 1830. The flag is a horizontal tricolour of yellow over blue over red. The blue and red bands each occupy one fourth of the flag's depth. Yellow stands for sovereignty and justice; blue for nobility, loyalty and vigilance; and red for courage, honour, and victory achieved by sacrifice. Yellow also represents universal liberty, blue the equality of all races, and red fraternity.

VENEZUELA

The Bolivarian Republic of Venezuela

Flag proportions: 2:3
Adopted: 20 April 1936
Capital: Caracas
Area: 912,050km² (352,144sq mi)
Population: 27,483,000
Language: Spanish

Religion: Roman Catholic
Currency: Bolívar
Exports: Petroleum and
petroleum products, basic metals,
steel, chemicals, agricultural
products (particularly meat).

Columbus explored the area in 1498, and it was settled by Spain in 1520. The original flag, an equal tricolour of yellow over blue over red, was created by Francisco de Miranda, who freed the country from the Spanish province of New Granada in 1806. Following a rebellion against Spanish rule in 1811, Venezuela was part of the republic of Gran Colombia from 1819, until independence in 1830. The present flag has seven white stars at its centre. Each star represents a Venezuelan province that supported the fight against Spain. Blue represents liberty, red represents courage, and yellow is for the original federation of states.

GUYANA

Co-operative Republic of Guyana

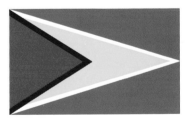

Flag proportions: 3:5
Adopted: 20 May 1966
Capital: Georgetown
Area: 215,083km² (83,044sq mi)
Population: 751,000
Language: English, English Creole

Religion: Hindu, Roman Catholic,
Sunni Islam
Currency: Guyana dollar
Exports: Sugar, gold, bauxite,
rice, shrimps, molasses, timber.

Guyana was ceded from Holland to Britain in 1814, becoming a British colony until independence in 1966, then a republic within the Common-wealth from 1970. The flag, known as the 'Golden Arrow', has five symbolic colours. Green is for agriculture and forestry, white for the perennial rivers, black for the people's endurance, red for the zeal and vigour of a young country, while the golden arrow itself represents mineral wealth. The designer of the flag, Whitney Smith, chose green because more than 90 per cent of the country is covered with fields or forests, once the domain of the Arawak, Carib and Warrau Indians.

SURINAME

The Republic of Suriname

Atlantic Ocean

Venezuela

SURINAME

Guyana

Flag proportions: 2:3
Adopted: 25 November 1975
Capital: Paramaribo
Area: 163,270km² (63,039sq mi)
Population: 493,000
Language: Dutch, Sranantonga (Surinamese Creole),

Hindi, Javanese
Religion: Hindu, Roman Catholic, Sunni Islam
Currency: Suriname guilder
Exports: Alumina/bauxite, oil, timber, shrimps and fish, rice, bananas.

After the colony of Dutch Guiana gained independence as Suriname in 1975, it faced a series of coups before order was restored and democratic elections held in 1991. Red and green were the colours of Suriname's main political parties at the time of independence, while the yellow star depicts unity and a golden future. Although Suriname is home to people of several ethnic groups, notably those of Indonesian, Indian and African descent, a single star was chosen to represent unity and hope. The colours have been interpreted as representing fertility (green), justice and freedom (white) and progress and spiritual renewal (red).

FRENCH GUIANA

The département of Guyane

Atlantic Ocean

Suriname

FRENCH GUIANA

Brazil

Flag proportions: 2:3
Adopted: n/a
Capital: Cayenne
Area: 86,504km² (33,399sq mi)
Population: 181,000
Language: French, French

Creole, Portuguese
Religion: Roman Catholic
Currency: Euro
Exports: Shrimps, timber and wood products, gold, rum, clothing.

Settled by France in 1604, Guiana became a French possession in 1817, a *département* in 1946 and an administrative region in 1974. It was once notorious for its offshore penal colonies, but the shipment of convicts ceased after 1945. The European Space Agency launches communication satellites from Kourou. Fishing and forestry are important industries.

Much of the territory now in French Guiana was contested by France and Brazil. In the late 19th century, a group of French businessmen sponsored the 'republic' of Independent Guyana. The venture failed, although their flag briefly flew over the settlement at Counani.

PERU

Republic of Peru

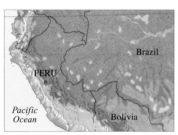

PERU

Pacific
Ocean

Brazil

Bolivia

Flag proportions: 2:3
Adopted: 25 February 1825
Capital: Lima
Area: 1,285,216km²
(496,225sq mi)
Population: 26,152,000
Languages: Spanish, Quechua

Religion: Roman Catholic, various
Evangelical Protestant churches
Currency: New Sol
Exports: Fish and fish products,
gold, copper, zinc, petroleum,
lead, coffee.

Peru's Inca Empire was vanquished by the Spanish conquistador Pizarro who, in 1533, executed the last Inca emperor. Peru became Spain's headquarters in South America and was the last country to receive independence, in 1826, after liberation by General José de San Martín. For his flag, he chose red and white to represent the Inca Empire and the rising sun. San Martín saw white as standing for peace and progress, and red as symbolizing courage and endeavour. On the arms are symbols of the animal, vegetable and mineral kingdoms. The palm and laurel wreaths around the shield are symbols of peace.

BRAZIL

Federative Republic of Brazil

BRAZIL

Bolivia

Flag proportions: 7:10
Adopted: 12 May 1992
Capital: Brasília
Area: 8,547,404km²
(3,300,171sq mi)
Population: 183,889,000
Language: Portuguese
Religion: Roman Catholic,

Pentecostal, Candomblé
Currency: Real
Exports: Transport equipment,
mineral ores (particularly iron ore),
iron and steel products, soybeans,
footwear and leather, machinery,
coffee, road vehicles, wood and
paper products, sugar.

A former Portuguese colony, Brazil became a kingdom in 1822 under King (later Emperor) Pedro I, and a republic in 1889. The blue sphere depicts the sky as seen from Rio de Janeiro at independence on 15 November 1889. Each star represents a state. The latest, added in 1992, makes 27 (with the Federal District). The constellations are accurate, and the size of the stars does not reflect the importance of the state. The motto, *Ordem e Progresso*, 'Order and Progress', is inscribed on a white band representing the equator. Green symbolizes the Amazon rainforest, and yellow, the rich mineral resources.

BOLIVIA
Republic of Bolivia

Flag proportions: 2:3
Adopted: 14 July 1880
Capitals: La Paz (administrative and legislative capital), Sucre (legal and constitutional capital)
Area: 1,098,581km² (424,165sq mi)
Population: 9,627,000

Language: Spanish, Quechua, Aymara
Religion: Roman Catholic, various Evangelical Protestant churches
Currency: Boliviano
Exports: Natural gas, soybeans, petroleum, zinc, gold, tin, timber.

Bolivia was part of the Inca Empire until it was conquered by Spain in 1538, becoming part of Peru. It stayed under Spanish rule until liberation by Simón Bolívar in 1825. By 1851, earlier versions of the flag had given way to the red-yellow-green horizontal tricolour. Red is for courage, yellow for mineral resources and green for fertility. At the centre the coat of arms comprises an oval enclosing symbols of the country's wealth, surrounded by weapons and banners in the national colours, surmounted by a condor. Bolivia has two capitals, Sucre and La Paz.

PARAGUAY
The Republic of Paraguay

Flag proportions: 3:5
Adopted: 27 November 1842
Capital: Asunción
Area: 406,752km² (157,048sq mi)
Population: 5,163,000
Language: Spanish, Guaraní

Religion: Roman Catholic
Currency: Guaraní
Exports: Soya flour and soyabeans, cattle feed, cotton, meat, electricity, oilseed and table oil, timber.

The flag of Paraguay, a former Spanish colony, has an obverse different to its reverse. Both sides have horizontal bands of red over white over blue. The colours represent patriotism and justice (red), unity and peace (white) and liberty (blue). On both sides, a central white disc is enclosed within blue and red circles. The obverse disc contains the state arms: a 'Star of May', recalling 1811, the date of independence, within a wreath of palm and laurel branches tied with red, white and blue ribbon, surrounded by the words *Republica del Paraguay*. The reverse bears the seal of the national treasury, a lion guarding a cap of liberty, and the motto 'Peace and justice'.

URUGUAY

The Oriental Republic of Uruguay

Flag proportions: 2:3
Adopted: 11 July 1830
Capital: Montevideo
Area: 176,215km²
(68,037sq mi)
Population: 3,306,000
Language: Spanish

Religion: Roman Catholic,
non-religious
Currency: Uruguayan peso
Exports: Meat, leather and
leather products, wool, fish, dairy
products.

The golden sun and stripes are adapted from the flags of Argentina and the USA respectively. The sun, a symbol of freedom, occupies the chief canton, while the field's equal horizontal stripes depict Uruguay's provinces. A Spanish colony until 1814, the territory was subsequently disputed by Argentina and Brazil, and annexed to both individually before gaining independence in 1830.

Uruguayan naval ships fly a flag of equal horizontal bands of blue-white-blue, with a diagonal red band rising from the hoist to the fly.

CHILE

Republic of Chile

Flag proportions: 2:3
Adopted: 18 October 1817
Capital: Santiago (administrative
and official capital), Valparaiso
(legislative capital)
Area: 756,626km² (292,135sq mi)
Population: 15,116,000
Language: Spanish

Religion: Roman Catholic, various
Evangelical Protestant churches
Currency: Chilean peso
Exports: Minerals (particularly
copper, iron ore, zinc, silver), fish
and fish products, fruit and
vegetables, paper and paper
products, chemicals, wine.

The first European to reach Chile was the Spanish explorer Ferdinand Magellan who, in 1520, sailed though the strait that now bears his name. Santiago, the capital, was established in 1541, and Chile remained under Spanish rule until independence in 1818. The 'lone star' Chilean flag was designed by Charles Wood, an American who fought alongside General José de San Martín to liberate Chile from Spain. Blue is for clear skies, white for the snow of the Andes, and red for the blood shed in the struggle for freedom. The white star is to guide the country towards progress and honour.

ARGENTINA

The Argentine Republic

Flag proportions: 2:3
Adopted: 12 February 1812
Capital: Buenos Aires
Area: 2,766,890km²
(1,068,302sq mi), excluding
territories claimed by Argentina
Population: 39,356,000

Language: Spanish
Religion: Roman Catholic
Currency: Argentine peso
Exports: Edible oils, petroleum
and petroleum products, cereals,
animal feed, motor vehicles,
meat, wool.

In 1810, Manuel Belgrano led mass demonstrations in support of liberation from Spain. He used a blue and white cockade to commemorate the 25 May uprising, when the clouds over Buenos Aires cleared to reveal the sun in a blue sky. The cockade became official in 1812 and the colours were adopted as a flag. Independence was achieved in 1816. In 1818, a golden radiant sun was added to recall the 1810 uprising. The sun is depicted with a face. It also features on the arms, along with the red cap of liberty.

Argentina has disputed claims to the Falkland Islands and parts of Antarctica.

FALKLAND ISLANDS

The Falkland Islands

Flag proportions: 1:2
Adopted: 1948, revised 1999
Capital: Stanley
Area: 12,170km² (4,698sq mi)
Population: 2,500

Language: English
Religion: Anglican
Currency: local issue of pound
sterling
Exports: Wool, hides, meat, fish.

The Falkland Islands' version of the Blue Ensign was granted in 1948. On the blue upper part of the arms, which are set on a shield, is a ram, underscoring the role wool plays in the island's economy. The wavy bands of blue and white on the base suggest the sea, on which is the *Desire*, the flagship of John Davis, who discovered the islands in 1592. Stars on the ship's sail represent the Southern Cross.

East and West Falkland, along with about 200 adjacent islets, are an overseas territory of the UK. After the 1982 Britain–Argentinian war over sovereignty, new port and airport facilities were opened in the capital, Stanley.

SOUTH GEORGIA AND THE SOUTH SANDWICH ISLANDS

South Georgia and the South Sandwich Islands

Atlantic Ocean

Falkland Islands

SOUTH GEORGIA AND THE SOUTH SANDWICH ISLANDS

Flag proportions: 1:2
Adopted: 2003
Main port: Grytviken
Area: 4,091km² (1,580sq mi)
Population: There is no permanent settlement
Language: English

Religion: n/a
Currency: n/a
Export: n/a

South Georgia and the South Sandwich Islands, some 1000km (600mi) southeast of the Falklands, are part of Antarctica, not South America. They were visited by Captain Cook in 1775 and annexed by Britain in 1908. The British Antarctic Survey has a base in Grytviken and a station on nearby Bird Island, but the South Sandwich Islands are uninhabited. The islands are administered from the Falklands, and a badge was granted to commemorate liberation after the 1982 war against Argentina. The blue and silver diamond pattern on the shield is described in heraldry as 'lozengy azure and argent', while the green wedge is known as a 'pile'. A lion rampant holds a flaming torch, symbolizing exploration. The supporters are a penguin and a seal.

AFRICA AND
ADJACENT ISLANDS

The African continent, covering an area of about 30 million km² (12 million sq mi), extends from the southern shores of the Mediterranean to Cape Agulhas, in South Africa. Natural resources include timber, gold and other rare metals, and diamonds in South Africa, Namibia and Botswana. There are large offshore reserves of oil reserves in Angola, while the Sahara Desert conceals large oil deposits.

Its late development is attributable to Africa's vast size and largely inhospitable terrain, over which transport was formerly impossible. Africa was the last major zone to be colonized by the Old World civilizations of Europe.

Portugal established tentative settlements along the newly discovered sea route to India in the early 16th century. By that time, outposts of the Turkish Ottoman Empire in North Africa were more than 200 years old. But it was the 19th century that generated 'the scramble for Africa', in which territory was claimed by, among others, Spain, Belgium, Germany, Italy, France and Britain.

British territory reached its greatest extent in the mid-20th century, after world wars deprived Italy and Germany of territorial claims. A wave of independence began in the 1950s and, by 1994, 'the last colony' – independent, white-ruled South Africa – had accepted a black-majority government, finally ending 'outsider' rule over Africa.

The Organization of African Unity was founded in 1963 to combat colonialism and promote African unity. By 2001 the African Union was established to enhance the economic, political and social integration and development of all African people. A new initiative is an acknowledgement by African leaders of the need to eradicate poverty and set their countries on a path of sustainable growth and development, while participating in the global economy and body politic.

AT A GLANCE

Biggest country: Sudan
Smallest country: Seychelles
Largest city: Cairo, Egypt
Major cities: Abidjan, Accra, Addis Ababa, Alexandria, Algiers, Brazzaville, Cape Town, Dakar, Dar es Salaam, Durban, Ibadan, Johannesburg, Kaduna, Kano, Khartoum, Kinshasa, Lagos, Luanda, Maputo, Nairobi, Pretoria, Rabat, Tunis, Tripoli.

Highest point: Mt Kilimanjaro, Tanzania 5895m (19,340ft)
Lowest point: Lac'Assal, Djibouti – 156m (512ft) below sea level).
Longest river: Nile, Uganda/Sudan/Egypt, 6,670km (4,145mi)
Largest lake: Victoria,Kenya/Uganda/Tanzania – 69,500km² (26,834sq mi).

Africa and adjacent islands

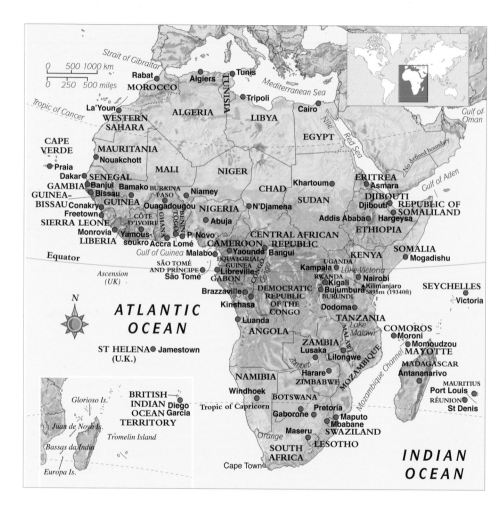

Strait of Gibraltar

0   500 1000 km
0   250 500 miles

Rabat
MOROCCO
Algiers
Tunis
TUNISIA
Mediterranean Sea
Tripoli
Cairo

Tropic of Cancer
La'Youn
WESTERN
SAHARA
ALGERIA
LIBYA
EGYPT
Nile
Red Sea
Gulf of Oman
No defined boundary

CAPE
VERDE
Praia
Dakar
MAURITANIA
Nouakchott
MALI
NIGER
ERITREA
Asmara
Gulf of Aden

GAMBIA
GUINEA-
BISSAU
Banjul
Bissau
Conakry
Bamako
BURKINA
FASO
Niamey
CHAD
Khartoum
DJIBOUTI
Djibouti
REPUBLIC OF
SOMALILAND
Hargeysa

SENEGAL
Freetown
SIERRA LEONE
GUINEA
Ouagadougou
NIGERIA
N'Djamena
SUDAN
Addis Ababa
ETHIOPIA

Monrovia
LIBERIA
CÔTE
D'IVOIRE
GHANA
TOGO
BENIN
Yamous-
soukro
Accra
Lomé
Abuja
P. Novo
CAMEROON
Yaounde
CENTRAL AFRICAN
REPUBLIC
Bangui
SOMALIA
Mogadishu

Equator
Gulf of Guinea
Malabo
EQUATORIAL
GUINEA
SÃO TOMÉ
AND PRÍNCIPE
São Tomé
Libreville
GABON
Congo
UGANDA
Kampala
Lake Victoria
KENYA
Nairobi
Kilimanjaro
5895m (19340ft)
SEYCHELLES
Victoria

Ascension
(UK)
Brazzaville
Kinshasa
DEMOCRATIC
REPUBLIC
OF THE
CONGO
RWANDA
Kigali
Bujumbura
BURUNDI
Dodoma

N
ATLANTIC
OCEAN
Luanda
ANGOLA
TANZANIA
MALAWI
Lake
Malawi
COMOROS
Moroni

ST HELENA
(U.K.)
Jamestown
ZAMBIA
Lusaka
Lilongwe
Harare
ZIMBABWE
Zambezi
MOZAMBIQUE
Momoudzou
MAYOTTE
MADAGASCAR
Antananarivo

NAMIBIA
Windhoek
Mozambique Channel
MAURITIUS
Port Louis
RÉUNION
St Denis

Glorioso Is.
BRITISH
INDIAN
OCEAN
TERRITORY
Diego
Garcia
Tropic of Capricorn
BOTSWANA
Gaborone
Pretoria
Maputo
Mbabane
SWAZILAND

Juan de Nova Is.
Tromelin Island
Maseru
LESOTHO

Bassas da India
Orange
SOUTH
AFRICA

Europa Is.
Cape Town
INDIAN
OCEAN

MOROCCO

The Kingdom of Morocco

Flag proportions: 2:3
Adopted: 17 November 1915
Capital: Rabat
Area: 446,550km² (172,413sq mi), excluding the Western Sahara territory; 712,550 km2 (275,115 sq. mi) including Western Sahara

Population: 29,475,000
Language: Arabic, Berber
Religion: Sunni Islam
Currency: Dirham
Exports: Clothing, fish, chemicals, phosphates, fertilizer, foodstuffs (fruit, wine and vegetables).

The red field proclaims the descent of Morocco's royal family from the Prophet Mohammed. Red was also used by the sherifs of the Holy City of Mecca and the imams of Yemen. At the centre of the flag, in green, is a pentagram. Known as the 'Seal of Solomon', it is an ancient symbol of life and health. The Seal is voided (depicted in outline) to show its construction. It was added to the flag, which for centuries had been plain red, when the French imposed a protectorate over the country. As a sign of mourning, the Moroccan flag has been tied around the mast rather than unfurled at half-mast. Morocco has annexed all of Western Sahara, which is now, de facto, part of Morocco (see page 184).

ALGERIA

The Democratic People's Republic of Algeria

Flag proportions: 2:3
Adopted: 3 July 1962
Capital: Algiers (El-Djazaïr)
Area: 2,381,741km² (919,595sq mi)
Population: 31,540,000

Language: Arabic, Tamazight (Berber)
Religion: Sunni Islam
Currency: Algerian dinar
Exports: Crude petroleum, natural gas, refined petroleum.

The flag is vertically divided into two equal bands of green and white, with green at the hoist. At the centre is a five-pointed red star within a red crescent, which faces towards the fly. Green is the traditional colour of Islam, while the crescent and star are symbols of the faith. White stands for purity and red symbolizes liberty and the sacrifices made in its attainment. The horns of the crescent are unusually long, to contain good fortune and happiness. Algeria was a French colony from 1830 until it achieved independence in 1962.

TUNISIA

The Republic of Tunisia

Flag proportions: 2:3
Adopted: 3 July 1999
Capital: Tunis
Area: 163,610km² (63,170sq mi)
Population: 10,126,000
Language: Arabic
Religion: Sunni Islam

Currency: Tunisian dinar
Exports: Textiles and clothing (and accessories), machinery and electrical apparatus, phosphates and chemicals, foodstuffs, petroleum and natural gas.

Tunisia was part of the Ottoman (Turkish) Empire from 1574 until 1881, when the country became a French Protectorate. Independence was granted in 1956 and Tunisia became a republic in 1957. In the 19th century, Tunisia wanted to assert its autonomy and, in 1835, the national flag on which the current design is based was adopted. The crescent and star are Islamic symbols, but the crescent alone was used in North Africa centuries before Islam arose. The waxing crescent moon is said to bring good fortune.

LIBYA

The Socialist People's Libyan Arab Jumhuriya

Flag proportions: 1:2
Adopted: 20 November 1977
Capital: Tripoli (Tarabulus) (official and diplomatic capital), Surt (legislative and administrative capital)
Area: 1,777,060km² (686,129sq mi)

Population: 6,098,000
Language: Arabic
Religion: Sunni Islam
Currency: Libyan dinar
Exports: Crude petroleum and refined petroleum products.

When the United Kingdom of Libya gained independence from Italy in 1951, the flag consisted of horizontal bands of red, black and green, with a white crescent and star at the centre, representing the Libyan provinces of Fezzan, Cyrenaica and Tripolitania. In 1969, following a successful military coup led by Colonel Muammar al Qaddafi, the crescent and star were removed and the colours changed to red, white and black. The present flag was adopted in 1977, after Libya quit the tri-national Federation of Arab Republics (with Egypt and Syria) to become an Islamic Socialist state. Green is the traditional colour of Islam.

EGYPT

Arab Republic of Egypt

Flag proportions: 2:3
Adopted: 4 October 1984
Capital: Cairo (Al-Qahirah)
Area: 997,739km²
(385,229sq mi)
Population: 72,579,000
Language: Arabic
Religion: Sunni Islam,

Coptic Christian
Currency: Egyptian pound
Exports: Petroleum and
petroleum products, cotton yarn
and textiles and clothing, basic
manufactures, metal products,
chemicals.

Red, white and black are the Arab Liberation colours. The flag was used in 1952 by the liberation movement that deposed the king of Egypt. Red is for the struggle, white for the revolution and black for the end of oppression. When Egypt joined the United Arab Republic in 1958, the flag was charged with two green stars. When the Federation of Arab Republics was formed in 1972, the Hawk of Quraish replaced the stars. In 1984 the flag reverted to that of the 1952 liberation struggle. On the white band is a stylized gold eagle known as the 'Eagle of Saladin'.

MAURITANIA

The Republic of Mauritania

Flag proportions: 2:3
Adopted: 1 April 1959
Capital: Nouakchott
Area: 1,030,700km²
(398,000sq mi)
Population: 2,906,000

Language: Arabic, Wolof
Religion: Sunni Islam
Currency: Ouguiya
Exports: Iron ore, fish and fish
products, gold.

Yellow and green are Pan-African colours; green is also the colour of Islam. The green field of the Mauritanian flag has been described as symbolizing hope, while yellow represents the sands of the Sahara Desert.

On this flag, the crescent and star emblem are unusual in that the crescent is depicted pointing upward. The same pattern is repeated on the national seal of this Islamic republic, together with other elements.

SENEGAL

The Republic of Senegal

Flag proportions: 2:3
Adopted: September 1960
Capital: Dakar
Area: 196,712km²
(75,951sq mi)
Population: 10,818,000
Language: French, Wolof, Fulani

Religion: Sunni Islam
Currency: CFA franc
Exports: Fish and crustaceans,
peanuts, and peanut oil,
phosphates, petroleum products,
cotton.

With the exception of the green star at its centre, the Senegalese flag is identical to that of Mali, as the two former French colonies were briefly united. The Pan-African colours of green, yellow and red were first used by Ethiopia and Ghana, and the star is said to represent unity and hope. In Senegal, the colours also represented the three political parties that merged to form the Senegalese Progressive Union of President Leopold Senghor. The star represents light and knowledge, and occurs frequently in African symbolism.

THE GAMBIA

The Republic of The Gambia

Flag proportions: 2:3
Adopted: 18 February 1965
Capital: Banjul
Area: 10,689km² (4,127sq mi)
Population: 1,365,000
Languages: English, Malinke,
Fulani, Wolof

Religion: Sunni Islam
Currency: Dalasi
Exports: Peanuts and peanut
products, fish and fish products,
cotton lint, processed food,
re-exports.

A former British colony, The Gambia obtained self-government in 1963, achieved independence as a constitutional monarchy within the Commonwealth in 1965 and became a republic in 1970. The flag adopted at independence was designed by Mr L Tomasi. There is more than one interpretation of the colours, but none are political. The simplest description is that the blue band represents the River Gambia as it flows through the green equatorial forests and the red soils of the savannah. The country lies on either side of the Gambia River.

154

CAPE VERDE

The Republic of Cape Verde

Flag proportions: 10:17
Adopted: 25 February 1992
Capital: Praia
Area: 4,033km² (1,557sq mi)
Population: 476,000
Language: Portuguese, Crioulo

(Portuguese Creole)
Religion: Roman Catholic
Currency: Cape Verde escudo
Exports: Re-exported fuel, shoes, clothing and textiles, fish and fish products, salt, bananas.

Cape Verde was settled by the Portuguese in the 15th century. When it gained independence in 1975, there was a move towards linking it with Guinea (now Guinea-Bissau), and so the two countries initially used similar flags. (There was insufficient support for this move, however.) The current flag came into being after the first multiparty elections brought a new government to power in 1992. Now a flourishing democracy, the government seeks close ties with the EU.

The circle of yellow stars depicts the archipelago's ten main islands in unity and without domination. Blue is for the Atlantic Ocean and for the sky, red is the road to progress and reconstruction and the effort that must be expended to follow it, and white is for peace.

GUINEA

The Republic of Guinea

Flag proportions: 2:3
Adopted: 10 November 1958
Capital: Conakry
Area: 245,857km²
(94,926sq mi)
Population: 9,030,000
Language: French, Fulani,

Malinke
Religion: Sunni Islam, Roman Catholic
Currency: Guinean franc
Exports: Bauxite, alumina, gold, diamonds, coffee, fish.

Guinea was part of a Muslim empire, centred on Mali, which flourished until the 15th century. Colonization by France, Britain and Portugal established the slave trade by the mid-15th century. In 1958, French Guinea became independent as Guinea, adopting a red-green-yellow flag. Guinea's first president, Sékou Touré, explained: 'red is the colour of blood, symbol of anticolonialist martyrs; the sweat of farmers and factory workers; and the wish for progress. Yellow is for Guinean gold and African sun, the source of energy, generosity and equality. Green symbolizes the countryside and prosperity, which comes from the soil, and the difficult life of our country's masses.'

GUINEA-BISSAU

The Republic of Guinea-Bissau

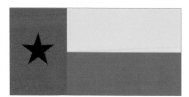

Flag proportions: 1:2
Adopted: 24 September 1973
Capital: Bissau
Area: 36,125km² (13,948sq mi)
Population: 1,296,000
Language: Portuguese, Crioulo

(Portuguese Creole), Balante
Religion: Traditional beliefs,
Sunni Islam
Currency: CFA franc
Exports: Cashew nuts, shrimps,
fish, peanuts, timber.

A slave-trading centre from 1446, Portuguese Guinea was administered with the Cape Verde islands until 1879, then as a separate colony until independence was negotiated in 1973, followed by the recognition of Guinea-Bissau as a sovereign nation in 1974. The flag adopted at independence has the full Pan-African colours of yellow, green, red and black, derived from the flag of Ghana. Red is for the blood shed in the struggle for independence, yellow represents the fruits of labour, and green is for the tropical forests and for hope. The five-pointed black star denotes African unity.

SIERRA LEONE

The Republic of Sierra Leone

Flag proportions: 2:3
Adopted: 27 April 1961
Capital: Freetown
Area: 71,740km² (27,699sq mi)
Population: 4,977,000
Language: English, Krio (English

Creole), Mende, Temne
Religion: Sunni Islam,
Traditional beliefs
Currency: Leone
Exports: Diamonds, rutile/titanium
ore, cocoa, coffee, fish.

Sierra Leone was founded as a home for freed slaves in 1787. It became a British colony in 1808, achieved independence in the Commonwealth in 1961 and became a republic in 1971. The flag is a horizontal tricolour of equal bands of green above white and blue. Blue represents the sea, white is for unity and justice, and green is for the country's natural resources.

Since 1991, civil war between the government and the Revolutionary United Front has resulted in the deaths of thousands and the displacement of over one-third of the population. UN-led efforts resulted in elections in 2002, and a UN peacekeeping force was in place until the end of 2005.

LIBERIA
The Republic of Liberia

Flag proportions: 10:19
Adopted: 26 July 1847
Capital: Monrovia
Area: 111,370km²
(43,000sq mi)
Population: 2,862,000
Language: English, Krio (English

Creole), Kpelle, Bassa
Religion: Traditional beliefs,
Sunni Islam
Currency: Liberian dollar and
US dollar
Exports: Rubber, timber, iron ore,
diamonds, cocoa, coffee.

Liberia was bought by the American Colonization Society as a home for freed slaves, the first of whom settled there in 1822.

'Lone star' is the familiar name for the flag, which traces its design to the US Stars and Stripes. The five-pointed white star, symbolizing African freedom, occupies a blue field in the chief canton. The field is made up of 11 horizontal stripes, six red and five white, representing the signatories to the 1847 declaration of Liberian independence. The colours have been described as blue for fidelity, red for valour, and white for purity.

CÔTE D'IVOIRE
The Republic of Côte d'Ivoire

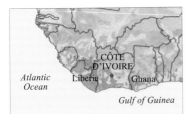

Flag proportions: 2:3
Adopted: 3 December 1959
Capital: Yamoussoukro (official
and legislative capital); Abidjan
(administrative and diplomatic
capital)
Area: 320,783km²
(123,854sq mi)
Population: 17,065,000

Language: French, Akan,
Malinké, Kru
Religion: Sunni Islam, Roman
Catholic, traditional beliefs
Currency: CFA franc
Exports: Cocoa, coffee, wood
and wood products, petroleum
products, cotton, bananas,
pineapples, palm oil.

The vertical tricolour resembles the *Tricolore* of France, the former colonial power. (Côte d'Ivoire was part of French West Africa before independence in 1960, and maintained an alliance with Niger for a period afterwards.) Orange is for the grasslands and the blood of a young people fighting for emancipation. White is for the rivers and for peace with justice. Green is for the coastal forests, for hope, and for the certainty of a better future. (The resemblance to the Irish flag is incidental.)

GHANA

The Republic of Ghana

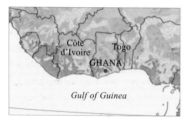

Côte
d'Ivoire
Togo
GHANA

Gulf of Guinea

Flag proportions: 2:3
Adopted: 6 March 1957
Capital: Accra
Area: 238,533km² (92,098sq mi)
Population: 8,845,000
Language: English, Hausa, Akan

Religion: Traditional beliefs, Sunni Islam, Roman Catholic
Currency: Cedi
Exports: Gold, cocoa, other food products (including tuna), timber, bauxite, aluminium, manganese.

Ghana, formerly Gold Coast, was the first British colony in Africa to gain independence, and its flag was copied by other former colonies. Ghana's black star came from the emblem of the Black Star shipping company, founded in 1919 by Marcus Garvey, a Jamaican nationalist. Red, yellow and green (from the Ethiopian flag) plus black created what became known as the 'Pan-African colours'. Red represents blood shed for independence, yellow the wealth of the country, and green the natural environment. The colours are those of the Rastafarian movement, which is based on Garvey's ideas.

TOGO

The Republic of Togo

Benin
TOGO
Ghana

Gulf of Guinea

Flag proportions: 2:3
Adopted: 27 April 1960
Capital: Lomé
Area: 56,785km² (21,925sq mi)
Population: 5,337,000
Language: French, Ewe, Kabre

Religion: Traditional beliefs, Roman Catholic, Sunni Islam
Currency: CFA franc
Exports: Re-exported goods, cotton, phosphates, coffee, cocoa.

The German protectorate of Togoland was divided between Britain and France after World War I. Britain's portion was incorporated with Ghana, and the French part gained independence, as Togo, in 1960. Official publications describe the flag: 'Red is for patriotic blood shed in the defence of integrity and sovereignty against aggressors. Green symbolizes nature, hope that represents Togo rising from colonization, and the dawn of a new era. Yellow is for unity and a common destiny. White is for peace, wisdom and dignity. The star is for liberty, life and the strength necessary for the people's development. The five bands represent strength and action in overcoming obstacles.'

BENIN

The Republic of Benin

Flag proportions: 2:3
Adopted: 1 August 1990
Capital: Porto Novo (official and legislative capital); Cotonou (de facto administrative and diplomatic capital)
Area: 112,622km² (43,484sq mi)

Population: 7,841,000
Language: French, Fon, Yoruba
Religion: Traditional beliefs, Roman Catholic, Sunni Islam
Currency: CFA franc
Exports: Cotton and cotton yarn, petroleum, palm products, cocoa.

From the 17th to the 19th centuries, the kingdom of Dahomey, as Benin was then known, was active in the slave trade. A former French colony, Benin became self-governing in 1958 and independent in 1960. The flag adopted then had equal horizontal bands of yellow above red, with a vertical green band at the hoist. Green stands for the hope of renewal, red for the ancestors' courage, and yellow for natural riches. As Pan-African colours, they also represent unity and nationalism. Following the establishment of a Marxist-based People's Republic in 1975, a plain green flag with a red star in the canton was used. The original flag was restored in 1990 after a referendum favoured a return to multiparty politics.

MALI

The Republic of Mali

Flag proportions: 2:3
Adopted: 1 March 1961
Capital: Bamako
Area: 1,248,574 km² (482,077sq mi)
Population: 11,732,000

Language: French, Bambara
Religion: Sunni Islam, traditional beliefs
Currency: CFA franc
Exports: Cotton and cotton products, gold, live animals.

A former French colony, Mali achieved independence in 1960, forming a short-lived confederation with neighbouring Senegal. The vertical tricolour in the Pan-African colours of green, yellow and red is based on the French *Tricolore*. The original flag bore a black stylized human figure, known as a *kanaga*, which was dropped in 1961. Green is for the natural environment, yellow for purity and mineral resources, and red for courage and sacrifice in the cause of independence.

BURKINA FASO

Burkina Faso

Flag proportions: 2:3
Adopted: 4 August 1984
Capital: Ouagadougou
Area: 274,122km²
(105,839sq mi)
Population: 13,730,000

Language: French, Mossi, Fulani
Religion: Sunni Islam, traditional
beliefs
Currency: CFA franc
Exports: Cotton, live animals,
gold, hides and skins.

Red symbolizes the revolution against French colonizers, and the star its guiding principles, while green represents the land's abundance of natural riches. Red, yellow and green are also the Pan-African colours. When the country achieved self-government in 1958 (as Upper Volta), the flag was a horizontal tricolour of black, white and red, representing the three major tributaries of the Volta River. The present colours were chosen as being more strongly expressive of solidarity with other former colonies in Africa.

NIGER

The Republic of Niger

Flag proportions: 6:7
Adopted: 23 November 1959
Capital: Niamey
Area: 1,186,408km²
(458,075sq mi)
Population: 11,060,000
Language: French, Hausa,

Djerma-Songhai, Fulani
Religion: Sunni Islam, traditional
beliefs
Currency: CFA franc
Exports: Uranium, livestock and
meat, cowpeas, onions.

On Niger's horizontal tricolour, the orange band is said to signify the country's savanna grasslands, while the disc at the centre represents the sun. White symbolizes the great Niger River, green the country's plains and rainforests. Other interpretations are that orange is for the Sahara Desert, green for fraternity, and white for purity and hope. The orange disc is sometimes interpreted as signifying sacrifices made by the people in their struggle to uphold justice and human rights.

The flags of Niger and Côte d'Ivoire are similar as they were designed in 1958, when both countries had an informal alliance with Chad and Dahomey (Benin). Niger achieved independence in 1960.

NIGERIA

The Federal Republic of Nigeria

Flag proportions: 1:2
Adopted: 1 October 1960
Capital: Abuja
Area: 923,103km² (356,411sq mi)
Population: 140,003,000
Language: English, English Creole, Hausa, Yoruba, Ibo, Fulani

Religion: Sunni Islam, traditional beliefs, Anglican, Roman Catholic, African Churches
Currency: Naira
Exports: Petroleum and petroleum products, cocoa, rubber.

From the 12th to the 14th century, Nigeria was home to the Yoruba and Ife cultures. English and Portuguese slave traders were active from the 15th century. In 1881 a British trader bought Lagos from a local chief. Further acquisitions resulted in Nigeria becoming Britain's largest West African colony. It became a federation in 1954, and achieved independence in 1960 as a constitutional monarchy within the Commonwealth. The green-white-green vertical tricolour was adopted at independence. The designer, Michael Akinkunmi, described green as representing the land and agriculture, with white for peace and unity.

CHAD

The Republic of Chad

Flag proportions: 2:3
Adopted: 6 November 1959
Capital: N'Djamena
Area: 1,284,000km² (495,755sq mi)
Population: 7,799,000
Languages: French, Arabic, Sara

Religion: Sunni Islam, Roman Catholic, traditional beliefs
Currency: CFA franc
Exports: Oil, cotton, live cattle, meat and animal hides, gum arabic.

The pattern and colours derive from the *Tricolore* of France (the former colonial power) and the Pan-African colours. Blue represents the sky, hope, and agriculture in the southern part of the land. Yellow is for the northern deserts and the sun. Red is for prosperity, unity and the readiness of citizens to make sacrifices for their country. Chad was settled by Arabs in the 7th century, before being conquered by Sudan. A province of French Equatorial Africa from 1913, Chad became an autonomous republic in 1958 and achieved independence in 1960. Since then, the flag has not been altered, despite unrest and regime changes. Unintentionally, Chad's flag is identical to Romania's.

CAMEROON

The Republic of Cameroon

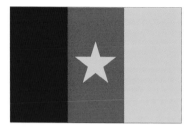

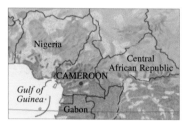

Flag proportions: 2:3
Adopted: 20 May 1975
Capital: Yaoundé
Area: 476,077km² (183,813sq mi)
Population: 15,881,000
Languages: French, English, Fang

Religion: Traditional beliefs, Roman Catholic, Sunni Islam
Currency: CFA franc
Exports: Crude petroleum, timber, cocoa beans, coffee, aluminium, cotton.

Cameroon's flag comprises Pan-African colours. A former German colony, it was partitioned between Britain and France after World War I. A plain green, red and yellow flag, based on the *Tricolore*, was first used in 1957. When Southern Cameroon joined French Cameroon in 1961, two yellow stars were placed in the the upper part of the green band. With a change of government in 1972, the stars were replaced with a single yellow star in the red band, representing unity between the north and south. Green stands for hope, as well as the natural vegetation, and yellow for prosperity, the soil and the sun.

CENTRAL AFRICAN REPUBLIC

The Central African Republic

Flag proportions: 2:3
Adopted: 1 December 1958
Capital: Bangui
Area: 622,436km² (240,324sq mi)
Population: 3,895,000
Languages: French, Sangho, Baya
Religion: Traditional beliefs,

Baptist, Roman Catholic, Sunni Islam
Currency: CFA franc
Exports: Diamonds, timber and timber products, cotton, coffee, tobacco.

The former French colony of Ubangi-Shari became the Central African Republic on independence in 1960. Adopted in 1958, the flag's design combines French and Pan-African colours. Four horizontal bands of blue, white, green and yellow are bisected by a central vertical red band. On the blue band is a yellow star. It has been said the red band symbolizes the people's willingness to shed blood for their country. Red also admonishes Europeans and Africans to respect one another. Blue represents freedom and serenity. Green is the colour of hope and faith, white is for dignity and equality, and yellow for tolerance and charity. The star forecasts a bright future.

EQUATORIAL GUINEA

The Republic of Equatorial Guinea

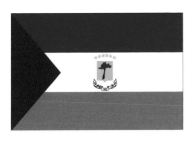

Gulf of Guinea · Cameroon · EQUATORIAL GUINEA · Gabon · Atlantic Ocean

Flag proportions: 2:3
Adopted: 21 August 1979
Capital: Malabo
Area: 28,051km² (10,831sq mi)
Population: 1,015,000

Language: Spanish, Fang
Religion: Roman Catholic
Currency: CFA franc
Exports: Petroleum products and methanol, timber, cocoa.

This tiny country incorporates five offshore islands. The islands came under Spanish rule in the mid-19th century, followed by the mainland territory of Río Muni (now Mbini) in 1885. The colony, known as Spanish Guinea, was a Spanish Overseas Province from 1959 until independence in 1968.

The horizontal tricolour of equal bands of green above white and red has a blue triangle at the hoist, its base occupying the full depth of the flag. Blue represents the sea that links the mainland and the islands, green is for the country's forests and natural resources, white is for peace, and red symbolizes the struggle for independence from Spain.

SÃO TOMÉ AND PRÍNCIPE

The Democratic Republic of São Tomé and Príncipe

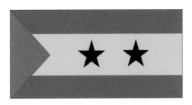

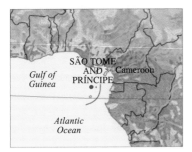

Gulf of Guinea · SÃO TOMÉ AND PRÍNCIPE · Cameroon · Atlantic Ocean

Flag proportions: 1:2
Adopted: 5 November 1975
Capital: São Tomé
Area: 1,001km² (386sq mi)
Population: 138,000
Language: Portuguese,

Portuguese Creole (Lungwa São Tomé)
Religion: Roman Catholic
Currency: Dobra
Exports: Cocoa, copra, coffee, palm oil.

The country comprises two main islands, São Tomé and Príncipe, plus several smaller islands in the Gulf of Guinea. Uninhabited until the arrival of the Portuguese in 1471, the islands played a role in the slave trade. The colony was given self-government in 1973, leading to independence in 1975.

A horizontal yellow band, half the depth of the flag, is enclosed top and bottom by equal bands of green. A red isosceles triangle is placed at the hoist. Two five-pointed black stars, representing the main islands, complete the Pan-African colours. Red represents blood shed for freedom, and green the forests, while yellow is for cocoa.

GABON

The Republic of Gabon

Flag proportions: 3:4
Adopted: 9 August 1960
Capital: Libreville
Area: 267,667km² (103,347sq mi)
Population: 1,322,000
Language: French, Fang

Religion: Roman Catholic, traditional beliefs
Currency: CFA franc
Exports: Petroleum and petroleum products, wood, manganese ore, uranium.

First visited by Portuguese slave traders in the 15th century, Gabon became part of the French Congo, and was a province of French Equatorial Africa from 1908. Virtually the whole country is covered with tropical rainforest, and its reserves of uranium, manganese and iron make Gabon one of the richest countries in central Africa. The flag adopted at independence in 1960 has the unusual proportions of 3:4 (most flags are 2:3). The colours are described as yellow and green for the country's natural resources, especially timber, and blue for the sea.

CONGO-BRAZZAVILLE

The Republic of the Congo

Flag proportions: 2:3
Adopted: 10 June 1991
Capital: Brazzaville
Area: 342,000km²
(132,047sq mi)
Population: 3,397,000
Language: French, Monokutuba, Kongo

Religion: Traditional beliefs, Roman Catholic
Currency: CFA franc
Exports: Petroleum and petroleum products, wood and timber products (including plywood), sugar, cocoa, coffee, diamonds.

The area came under French administration in 1889, and was part of French Equatorial Africa from 1910. The Congo became an autonomous republic in 1958, and achieved independence in 1960. After a Marxist revolution in 1964, the country became the People's Republic of the Congo in 1970. The present flag, first used in 1959, was retained after independence. With the formation of the People's Republic a new flag was introduced, consisting of the national emblem in the chief canton, on a field of red. Marxism was abandoned in 1990, and the original flag was restored. Its colours are Pan-African.

DEMOCRATIC REPUBLIC OF THE CONGO

The Democratic Republic of the Congo

Flag proportions: 2:3
Adopted: 2006
Capital: Kinshasa
Area: 2,344,856km²
(905,354sq mi)
Population: 58,300,000
Language: French, Lingala,

Swahili, Kongo
Religion: Roman Catholic, African
Churches (mainly Zimbanguists),
Anglican, traditional beliefs
Currency: Congolese franc
Exports: Diamonds, copper,
coffee, cobalt, crude petroleum.

From 1885 to independence in 1960, the Belgian Congo used a blue flag with a central yellow star. At independence, a row of six yellow stars was added at the hoist to signify the provinces at the time. Changes of government resulted in three new flags between 1963 and 1996, and the name Zaire being used from 1971 to 1997. In 2006, the Democratic Republic of the Congo adopted a new flag: a variant of the flag flown from 1963 to 1997, with a light blue field (representing hope) and a red stripe (symbolizing blood shed for freedom) lined with narrow gold bars (representing prosperity). The star in the canton represents unity.

RWANDA

The Republic of Rwanda

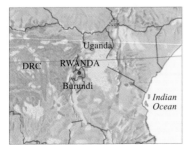

Flag proportions: 1:2
Adopted: 31 December 2001
Capital: Kigali
Area: 26,338km² (10,169sq mi)
Population: 8,129,000
Language: Rwanda, French,

English, Swahili
Religion: Roman Catholic,
traditional beliefs
Currency: Rwanda franc
Exports: Coffee, tea, hides and
skins, tin.

Rwanda came under Belgian administration after 1919, and gained independence in 1962. In 1959, fighting between the majority ethnic Hutus and rival Tutsis sent thousands of Tutsis into exile. In 1990, the children of these exiles formed the Rwandan Patriotic Front, beginning a civil war that culminated in the 1994 genocide of ±800,000 Tutsis and moderate Hutus, with refugees fleeing to neighbouring countries. Most have since returned but, despite 1999 elections, tensions remain. The flag comprises a half-depth band of blue above yellow and green bands. A sun symbolizes enlightenment, leading to unity. Blue is for hope and the promise of peace, green is for prosperity, yellow for the need for reconstruction.

BURUNDI

The Republic of Burundi

Flag proportions: 2:3
Adopted: 27 September 1982
Capital: Bujumbura
Area: 27,834km² (10,759sq mi)
Population: 6,490,000
Language: Rundi, French, Swahili

Religion: Roman Catholic,
traditional beliefs, Sunni Islam
Currency: Burundi franc
Exports: Coffee, tea, sugar,
cotton, animal hides.

Burundi, a Belgian possession from 1919–1962, became an independent kingdom in 1962. The flag's emblems were a drum and a stalk of sorghum, but when the country became a republic in 1966 these were replaced by three red stars in a white disc at the centre of a white saltire. The stars represent the national motto and the main ethnic groups: Tutsi, Hutu and Twa. The saltire's arms create four triangles, the apexes clipped by the central disc. Those at the hoist and fly are green, the others are red. White is for hope, red for sacrifices made for independence, and green represents hope for a peaceful, prosperous future.

SUDAN

Republic of the Sudan

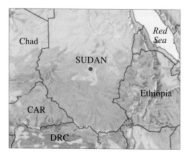

Flag proportions: 1:2
Adopted: 20 May 1970
Capital: Khartoum
Area: 2,505,815km²
(967,500sq mi)
Population: 37,239,000
Language: Arabic, Dinka, Nubian
languages

Religion: Sunni Islam, traditional
beliefs
Currency: Sudanese dinar
Exports: Petroleum, cotton,
foodstuffs (particularly sesame,
peanuts and sugar), livestock,
gum arabic.

Sudan was ruled jointly by Egypt and Britain until it became independent in 1956. After the formation of the Democratic Republic of Sudan in 1968, a national competition was held to choose a new flag, and the winning entry was adopted in 1970. Equal horizontal bands of red over white and black echo the flags of Egypt and other Arab countries, but Sudan adds a green isosceles triangle at the hoist. Red is for socialism and the blood shed for liberty, white is for peace and optimism, black is for the 19th-century ruler, Mahdi, who led a revolt against Egypt, and green symbolizes agriculture and Islamic prosperity.

ERITREA

Eritrea

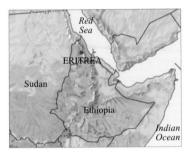

Flag proportions: 1:2
Adopted: 24 May 1993
Capital: Asmara
Area: 121,100km² (46,757sq mi)
Population: 3,622,000
Languages: Tigrinya, Arabic

Religion: Sunni Islam, Ethiopian Orthodox
Currency: Nakfa
Exports: Livestock and hides, sorghum, textiles, manufactures (including footwear).

Eritrea was part of the Ethiopian kingdom until the 7th century. It subsequently fell under Turkish, Italian and British rule before reverting to Ethiopia in 1962. The red, green and blue of the three triangles are the colours of the Eritrean People's Liberation Front (EPLF), which waged a lengthy campaign for independence from Ethiopia, finally obtaining it in 1993. Following independence, the EPLF emblem (a gold star) was replaced with a golden olive branch set within a wreath of olive leaves, to symbolize the winning of the country's autonomy.

DJIBOUTI

The Republic of Djibouti

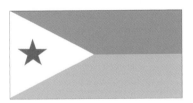

Flag proportions: 21:38
Adopted: 27 June 1977
Capital: Djibouti
Area: 23,200km² (8,950sq mi)
Population: 638,000
Languages: French, Arabic,

Somali, Afar
Religion: Sunni Islam
Currency: Djibouti franc
Exports: Re-exports, hides and skins, live animals.

Djibouti was formerly called French Somaliland and, later, the Territory of the Afars and Issas. Opposition to French rule grew in the 1970s, with frequent and sometimes violent clashes occuring until independence was achieved in 1977. The national flag is adapted from that of the former liberation movement, *Ligue Populaire Africaine pour l'Indépendance*. It is divided horizontally into equal bands of light blue over green, with a white equilateral triangle at the hoist. Blue represents the Issa people, and green the Afars – the two main ethnic groups. Within the triangle is a red star, a symbol of unity. White is for the peace eventually attained.

ETHIOPIA

Federal Democratic Republic of Ethopia

Flag proportions: 1:2
Adopted: 6 February 1996
Capital: Addis Ababa
Area: 1,127,127km²
(435,184sq mi)
Population: 75,067,000
Language: Amharic, Oromo,
Sidamo
Religion: Sunni Islam, Ethiopian
Orthodox, traditional beliefs
Currency: Birr
Exports: Coffee, qat, gold, leather
goods and animal hides, pulses
and oilseed.

Ethiopia's hereditary rulers, the last of whom was Emperor Haile Selassie (1892–1975), claimed descent from the biblical King David. The first flag's green-yellow-red tricolour once referred to the Holy Trinity. A more contemporary interpretation is green for hope, the land and fertility; yellow for peace and justice; and red for power, faith and sacrifice. The Seal of Solomon, added in 1996, signifies unity in diversity. Rays emanating from it symbolize prosperity, and the blue disc is for peace.

In the 1930s, the Ethiopian colours were adopted by Jamaicans who saw Africa as a spiritual homeland. With the addition of black, the colours now represent the Rastafarian movement.

SOMALIA

Somalia

Flag proportions: 2:3
Adopted: 12 October 1954
Capital: Mogadishu, but Baidoa
has been the temporary seat of
the parliament and government
since 2006
Area: 637,657km² (246,201sq
mi), including Somaliland
Population: 8,590,000,
including Somaliland
Language: Somali, Arabic
Religion: Sunni Islam
Currency: Somali shilling
Exports: Livestock, bananas, hides.

Somalia went through British and Italian rule and UN trusteeship prior to independence in 1960, and adopted its flag when the territory was under UN administration. Set on a field of UN blue, a five-pointed star represents countries where the Somali people traditionally lived.

Somalia has been in a state of civil war since 1991. A transitional government was put in place in 2000, and in 2004 a president was elected. Fighting broke out in 2006 between the US-backed warlords and the Islamist militias, who expelled the warlords from the capital. In 2007 the government drove the militias from Mogadishu and southern Somalia, but by the year end the government had lost control of most of its territory.

KENYA

The Republic of Kenya

Flag proportions: 2:3
Adopted: 12 December 1963
Capital: Nairobi
Area: 582,646km²
(224,961sq mi)
Population: 33,947,000
Languages: Swahili, English

Religion: Roman Catholic, African Christian Churches, traditional beliefs
Currency: Kenya shilling
Exports: Tea, fruit and vegetables, coffee, petroleum products, fish, cement.

Parts of the region were inhabited by early humans over five million years ago. The coast was settled by Arab traders in the 8th century and fell under Portuguese rule in the 15th century. The country became a British protectorate in 1896 and a colony in 1921. Kenya gained independence in 1963 and joined the Commonwealth in 1964. Black, red and green are the Kenya African National Union's colours. On the flag they are separated by white stripes, representing democracy, peace and unity. Black represents the majority of the people, red is for sacrifice, and green for natural resources. A Masai shield and two crossed spears symbolize readiness to defend freedom.

UGANDA

The Republic of Uganda

Flag proportions: 2:3
Adopted: 9 October 1962
Capital: Kampala
Area: 241,040km²
(93,072sq mi)
Population: 27,357,000
Language: Swahili, English, Ganda

Religion: Roman Catholic, Anglican, traditional beliefs, Sunni Islam
Currency: Uganda shilling
Exports: Coffee, fish and fish products, tea, gold, cotton, cut flowers, vegetables.

Uganda gained independence from Britain in 1962 as part of the Commonwealth. By 1971, following a series of coups, it was under the dictatorial regime of Major-General Idi Amin Dada, who suspended the constitution and took absolute power. He was overthrown in 1978, but Uganda remained in a state of unrest until the establishment of a broad-based coalition government in 1986. The flag adopted in 1962 was based on the tricolour of the dominant Uganda People's Congress. The colours symbolize the people (black), sunlight (yellow) and brotherhood (red). Uganda's national bird, the crested crane, is depicted on a central white disc. Despite regime changes, the flag has endured.

TANZANIA

The United Republic of Tanzania

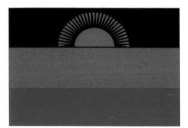

Flag proportions: 2:3
Adopted: 30 June 1964
Capital: Dodoma (legislative capital and official capital); Dar es Salaam (administrative capital)
Area: 945,037km²
(364,881sq mi)
Population: 34,444,000

Language: Swahili, English, Nyamwezi
Religion: Traditional beliefs, Sunni Islam, Roman Catholic
Currency: Tanzania shilling
Exports: Gold, coffee, cashew nuts, manufactured goods, cotton, tobacco.

The flag represents the union of the former British Tanganyika and Zanzibar, whose long-ruling Sultanate was overthrown in 1964. Zanzibar's flag was a horizontal tricolour of blue above black and green, while that of Tanganyika had a green field equally divided by a horizontal, gold-edged black band. The flag of the United Republic of Tanzania combines elements of both. Green symbolizes the land and blue the sea, while gold is for mineral wealth and black for the people.

Tanzania's attractions include Africa's highest mountain, Kilimanjaro 5,895m (19,340ft), and Stone Town, on Zanzibar, a UN World Heritage Site.

MALAWI

The Republic of Malawi

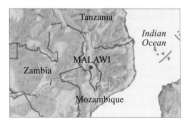

Flag proportions: 2:3
Adopted: 6 July 1964
Capital: Lilongwe
Area: 118,484km²
(45,747sq mi)
Population: 13,188,000
Languages: English,

Chichewa, Lomwe
Religion: Sunni Islam, Roman Catholic, Presbyterian
Currency: Malawi Kwacha
Exports: Tobacco, tea, sugar, cotton. coffee, peanuts, wood.

Midway along the uppermost band of the horizontal tricolour of Malawi is a representation of a radiant rising sun, or kwacha, in red, symbolizing a new dawn of hope and progress in Africa. The role of the sun is underscored by the fact that Malawi's currency is termed the Kwacha. At independence in 1964, the colours chosen were those of the dominant Malawi Congress Party. Black represents the people and their heritage, red is the colour of sacrifice, while green represents the land and its natural resources.

ANGOLA

The Republic of Angola

Flag proportions: 2:3
Adopted: 11 November 1975
Capital: Luanda
Area: 1,246,700km²
(481,354 sq mi)
Population: 15,566,000
Language: Portuguese,
Umbundu, Kimbundu, Kongo
Religion: Traditional religions,
Roman Catholic
Currency: New Kwanza
Exports: Petroleum and
petroleum products, diamonds,
gas, coffee, fish and fish products.

Angola's constitution decrees that its flag be divided into red and black horizontal bands. Black represents Africa, red is the blood shed for liberation and yellow is for wealth. The cogwheel symbolizes workers and industry; the machete is for peasants, agriculture and the armed struggle; and the star for international solidarity. The design is based on the former Soviet flag, but Angola has abandoned Marxism, raising the possibility of a new flag.

After a civil war to end Portuguese rule, the People's Liberation Movement took power in 1975. Unrest continued until 1994, when government and rebel (UNITA) forces integrated. The fighting resumed in 1998, but ended with a ceasefire in 2002.

ZAMBIA

The Republic of Zambia

Flag proportions: 2:3
Adopted: 24 October 1964
Capital: Lusaka
Area: 752,614km²
(290,586sq mi)
Population: 9,886,000
Language: English, Bemba, Tonga
Religion: Traditional African
beliefs, Roman Catholic, Anglican
Currency: Zambian Kwacha
Exports: Copper, cobalt,
electricity, tobacco, cut flowers,
cotton.

The charges depicted on the flag are placed at the fly rather than the hoist. In the lower corner a vertical red-black-orange tricolour represents, respectively, the struggle for independence, the people, and the country's mineral wealth. The colours are also those of the dominant political party at independence in 1964. In the upper fly, an eagle represents liberty and freedom. The green field signifies the land's natural resources. As the former British colony of Northern Rhodesia, Zambia was part of the Federation of Rhodesia and Nyasaland (now Malawi), and it remains in the Commonwealth. The southern border is the Zambezi River, on which the Victoria Falls are situated.

ZIMBABWE

The Republic of Zimbabwe

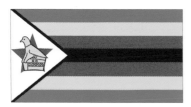

Flag proportions: 1:2
Adopted: 18 April 1980
Capital: Harare
Area: 390,757km²
(150,872sq mi)
Population: 11,635,000
Language: English, Shona,
Ndebele

Religion: Syncretic beliefs (part-
traditional; part-Christian),
traditional beliefs, Roman Catholic
Currency: Zimbabwe dollar
Exports: Tobacco, gold,
ferroalloys and nickel, cotton
textiles and clothing, cut flowers.

After years of UN sanctions and a protracted civil war, the former British colony of Rhodesia became Zimbabwe in 1980. Since independence, the once-prosperous country has slid into economic and political chaos under Robert Mugabe. The green, yellow, red and black of the ruling Zimbabwe African National Union (ZANU) appear as equal horizontal stripes. A white isosceles triangle, its base at the hoist, occupies the full depth. It points to a peaceful future, while the black border represents the postcolonial leadership and a five-pointed red star symbolizes Marxism. The yellow Zimbabwe bird is based on stone carvings from centuries-old local ruins.

MOZAMBIQUE

Republic of Mozambique

Flag proportions: 2:3
Adopted: 1 May 1983
Capital: Maputo
Area: 801,590km²
(309,496sq mi)
Population: 20,530,000
Language: Portuguese,

Makua, Tsonga
Religion: Traditional beliefs, Sunni
Islam, Roman Catholic
Currency: Metical
Exports: Aluminium, prawns and
shrimps, cotton, cashew nuts,
sugar, citrus fruits.

The flag's colours come from Frelimo, the leading political party. Red symbolizes resistance to colonialism, green the land's richness, black the African continent, yellow the mineral riches, and white peace and justice. The rifle stands for vigilance in defence, the hoe is for agriculture, the book for education. The yellow star is for Marxism. Mozambique is one of the poorest countries in Africa, its poverty exacerbated by drought and a protracted civil war. Economic reforms, including abandoning Marxism in 1989, have resulted in improvements. However, despite a ceasefire in 1992 and free multi-party elections in 1995, much of the population still lives below the poverty line.

NAMIBIA

The Republic of Namibia

Flag proportions: 2:3
Adopted: 21 March 1990
Capital: Windhoek
Area: 824,269km²
(318,250sq mi)
Population: 1,830,000
Language: English,

Ovambo, Nama
Religion: Lutheran, Roman
Catholic
Currency: Namibian dollar
Exports: Diamonds, copper, gold,
zinc, lead, meat and cattle, fish
and fish products.

Namibia was part of Imperial Germany, Great Britain and South Africa prior to independence in 1990. The new flag comprises a field divided into two right-angled triangles by a diagonal red band, bordered with white, rising from the hoist. The green triangle symbolizes natural resources, while the blue triangle represents the sky, Atlantic Ocean, marine resources, and the importance of rain. White is for peace and unity, yellow for the Namib Desert, and red for future hopes. The colours came from the main political parties at independence. A gold sun depicts life and energy, its rays separated from the sun's body by a narrow blue circle.

BOTSWANA

The Republic of Botswana

Flag proportions: 2:3
Adopted: 30 September 1966
Capital: Gaborone
Area: 581,730km²
(224,606sq mi)
Population: 1,681,000
Languages: English,

Tswana, Shona
Religion: Traditional beliefs,
Roman Catholic
Currency: Pula
Exports: Diamonds, copper-
nickel, soda, meat, textiles.

Rain, a rare and precious commodity, is depicted on the Botswana flag by two equal horizontal bands of pale blue. In the desert, water is life, and the Setswana word *pula* means not only 'water' and 'rain', but also the life that is derived from it. The country's currency is the Pula, and the term forms the national motto as well. Between the blue bands is a narrow horizontal band of black bordered with white, symbolizing the harmonious coexistence of the country's large black population with the relatively small number of whites.

SOUTH AFRICA

Republic of South Africa

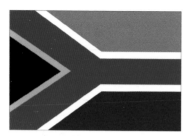

Flag proportions: 2:3
Adopted: 27 April 1994
Capital: Pretoria (administrative capital); Cape Town (legislative capital)
Area: 1,224,691km² (472,854sq mi)
Population: 46,888,000
Language: English, Afrikaans,
Zulu, Xhosa, Sotho languages
Religion: Traditional beliefs, African Christian Churches, Afrikaans Reformed Church
Currency: Rand
Exports: Gold, diamonds, platinum, other metals, machinery and equipment, foodstuffs.

Many flags have flown over South Africa in 350 years, and this legacy is reflected. Red, white and blue are from the Dutch and British flags; black, green and yellow are from the African National Congress. The Y-pattern symbolizes the merging of groups. From its establishment as a republic in 1961 to the first democratic elections in 1994, South Africa was fragmented between an economically powerful white minority and a disenfranchised black majority. Under Nelson Mandela the country united, but issues of poverty reduction and economic growth still prevail.

SWAZILAND

The Kingdom of Swaziland

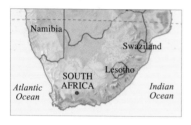

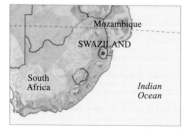

Flag proportions: 2:3
Adopted: 30 October 1967
Capital: Mbabane (administrative capital); Lobamba (royal and legislative capital)
Area: 17,363km² (6,704sq mi)
Population: 954,000
Languages: English, Swazi
Religion: Syncretic beliefs (part-traditional; part-Christian), Roman Catholic, Sunni Islam
Currency: Lilangeni
Exports: Soft drinks, sugar, wood and wood products, cotton.

Swaziland was a British protectorate until 1968. The flag is derived from one presented by King Sobhuza II to the Swazi contingent of the Africa Pioneer Corps in 1941. The blue bands represent peace after battles of the past (red); yellow is for natural resources. On the red band is a cowhide shield with two spears and a fighting stick with tassles, comprising feathers of the lourie and the widowbird. Another tassle is attached to the shield. Since 1968, Swaziland has been ruled by King Mswati III. A hereditary monarchy, political parties are banned, but there is pressure for political reform and the implementation of democratic representation.

LESOTHO

Kingdom of Lesotho

Flag proportions: 2:3
Adopted: 2006
Capital: Maseru
Area: 30,355km² (11,720sq mi)
Population: 2,158,000
Language: English, Sotho

Religion: Roman Catholic,
traditional beliefs, various
Evangelical Churches
Currency: Maluti
Exports: Clothing, footwear,
foodstuffs, live animals, wool.

Formerly Basutoland, Lesotho, a mountainous land, gained independence as a constitutional monarchy in 1966 and has been ruled by King Letsie III since 1990. In 2006, Lesotho adopted a new flag, the third since independence, but the basic colours of all three flags have been the same. These colours represent Lesotho's motto, *Khotso-Pula-Nala*: 'peace (white), rain (blue) and prosperity (green)'. The new flag is a horizontal tricolour of blue, white and green, and displays on the central white stripe the national symbol, a black Basuto hat.

MADAGASCAR

The Republic of Madagascar

Flag proportions: 2:3
Adopted: 21 October 1958
Capital: Antananarivo
Area: 587,041km²
(226,658sq mi)
Population: 15,692,000
Language: Malagasy, French

Religion: Traditional beliefs,
Roman Catholic, Protestant
Church of Madagascar
Currency: CFA franc
Exports: Coffee, vanilla, shrimps,
sugar, cotton, chromite, cloves.

The flag comprises equal horizontal bands of red above green, and a broad vertical band of white at the hoist. Red and white come from the pre-colonial Merina Kingdom, under which most of the country was united. Green is for the Hova people who comprise the agricultural peasant class. Madagascar became a French protectorate in 1885, achieved self-government in 1958 and independence in 1960. Martial law was imposed in 1975 under a Marxist constitution, which was abandoned in 1980. Elections in 1992–93 ended 17 years of single-party rule, but the hotly contested 2001 presidential election nearly caused secession of half the country.

COMOROS

The Union of the Comoros

Tanzania
Mozambique
COMOROS
Madagascar
Indian Ocean

Flag proportions: 2:3
Adopted: 23 December 2001
Capital: Moroni
Area: 1,862km² (719sq mi)
Population: 576,000
Language: Comorian or

Shikomoro, French, Arabic
Religion: Sunni Islam
Currency: Comorian franc
Exports: Vanilla, ylang-ylang,
cloves, perfume oil, copra.

Since gaining independence from France in 1975, there have been repeated coups or attempted coups by the islands of Mohéli/Mwali, Anjouan/Nzwani, Grand Comore/Njazidja and Mayotte, to give both their French and local names. Anjouan and Mohéli declared independence in 1997. Mayotte remains a territorial collectivity of France, although it is claimed by the Comoros. A new constitution was adopted in January 2002.

At the hoist, a green triangle bears a white crescent with a row of four stars between the tips. Both the crescent and green are emblems of Islam. The stars represent the larger islands, as do the equal horizontal stripes of yellow, white, red and blue.

MAYOTTE

Mayotte

Tanzania
Comoros
Mozambique
• MAYOTTE
Madagascar
Indian Ocean

Flag proportions: 2:3
Adopted: n/a
Capital: Mamoudzou
Area: 376km² (145sq mi)
Population: 160,000
Language: French, Mahorian

(Shimaoré)
Religion: Sunni Islam
Currency: Euro
Exports: Ylang-ylang, vanilla,
copra, coconuts, coffee,
cinnamon.

The island of Mayotte is part of the Comoros archipelago and, while it is a French overseas dependency, it is claimed by the Comoros. Like the other islands in the group, Mayotte became French in 1843. However, in 1974 and 1976 the people of Mayotte chose to remain French while the inhabitants of the other three Comoran islands opted for independence. Continued French rule in Mayotte is not recognized by many countries, but in 2009, the island's voters will take part in a plebiscite that will offer Mayotte the status of an overseas French departement. A local flag, used only on the island, is white, with Mayotte's coat-of-arms at the centre, supported by two sea horses and the island's name above.

SEYCHELLES
Republic of Seychelles

Flag proportions: 1:2
Adopted: 8 January 1996
Capital: Victoria, on Mahé
Area: 455km² (175sq mi)
Population: 83,000
Language: Creole,

English, French
Religion: Roman Catholic
Currency: Seychelles rupee
Exports: Fish, cinnamon, copra, refined oil products.

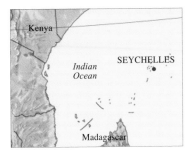

The Seychelles became a French colony in 1756 but were relinquished during the Napoleonic Wars when Britain sought to curb French colonial expansion. The Treaty of Paris confirmed British rule in 1814, and the Seychelles became a Crown Colony in 1903. Independence followed 73 years later on 29 June, when the new republic was declared.

The present flag was designed to effect reconciliation after the Seychelles became a multiparty democracy in 1993. The five bands radiating from the lower hoist represent the colours of two major political parties. Red, being common to both, is placed between white and green, for the ruling Seychelles People's United Party, and blue and yellow, for the opposition Democratic Party.

BRITISH INDIAN OCEAN TERRITORY
BIOT

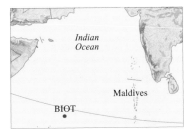

Flag proportions: 3:5
Adopted: 4 November 1990
Capital: None
Area: 60km² (23sq mi)
Population: No permanent settlement, but there is an estimated 2,000 US military

personnel and 2,000 Philippine civilian contractors on the island of Diego Garcia
Language: English
Religion: n/a
Currency: US dollar
Exports: n/a

The British Indian Ocean Territory comprises six main island groups in the Chagos Archipelago. Established in 1965, it provides a joint US–UK military presence in the Indian Ocean. Diego Garcia, the largest island, is home to a naval base. In 2000, a British High Court granted former residents, relocated to Mauritius and the Seychelles in the 1960s and '70s, the right to return (but not to Diego Garcia). They have not yet been able to do so. The flag is based on the Blue Ensign, with the local badge in the fly. Blue and white wavy lines represent the ocean, the palm tree shows the islands' vegetation and the Union Flag and crown symbolize British sovereignty.

RÉUNION

The département of Reunion

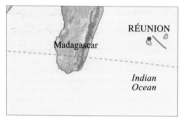

RÉUNION

Madagascar

Indian
Ocean

Flag proportions: 2:3
Adopted: n/a
Capital: Saint-Denis
Area: 2,510km² (969sq mi)
Population: 752,000
Language: French, French Creole

Religion: Roman Catholic,
Sunni Islam
Currency: Euro
Exports: Sugar, rum, molasses,
perfume essences, lobsters.

Réunion is an overseas department of France, so the official flag is the *Tricolore*. In 1642 the Mascarene Islands, which includes Réunion and Mauritius, were claimed by Louis XIII of France, but only Réunion is still French. During the 17th and 18th centuries, French settlers, Africans, Chinese, Malays and Malabar Indians established the rich ethnic mix that prevails today.

Mountainous Réunion is the site of an active volcano, Piton de la Fournaise, on the southeastern coast. The region is subject to periodic cyclones from December to April, and a cyclone centre at Saint-Denis acts as the monitoring station for the entire Indian Ocean.

MAURITIUS

Republic of Mauritius

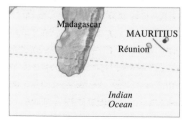

Madagascar

MAURITIUS

Réunion

Indian
Ocean

Flag proportions: 2:3
Adopted: 12 January 1968
Capital: Port Louis
Area: 2,040km² (788sq mi)
Population: 1,249,000
Language: English, French

Creole, Bhojpuri
Religion: Hindu, Roman Catholic,
Sunni Islam
Currency: Mauritius rupee
Exports: Clothing and textiles,
sugar, cut flowers, molasses.

The four equal horizontal bands recall the colours of the island's coat of arms. Red stands for independence, blue for the Indian Ocean, yellow is a symbol of a bright future, and green is for the lush vegetation. A French colony from 1715, Mauritius was siezed by Britain in 1810. African slaves worked in the sugar-cane plantations, but the abolition of slavery in 1833 saw the arrival of indentured labourers from India, whose descendents now constitute about 70 per cent of the population. Internal self-government in 1957 was followed by independence within the Commonwealth in 1968. Tourism is important to the economy.

SAINT HELENA

Saint Helena

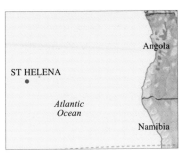

Flag proportions: 1:2
Adopted: Unknown
Capital: Jamestown
Area: 411km² (159sq mi)
Population: 5,500
Language: English

Religion: Anglican, Baptist, Seventh-day Adventist
Currency: Local issue of the British pound
Exports: Canned and frozen fish, coffee, handicrafts.

This tiny volcanic island became a British possession in 1673 and a colony in 1834, and remains one of Britain's overseas territories. The island flag, and also that of its dependencies, Ascension Island and the Tristan da Cunha group, is the British Blue Ensign with the arms of St Helena at the fly. The arms consist of a shield, on which is depicted a three-masted British warship, with furled sails, below a steep cliff. The ship is flying the Cross of St George. In the upper part of the shield, against a yellow field, is a wirebird, a species endemic to St Helena.

FRENCH SOUTHERN AND ANTARCTIC TERRITORIES

French Southern and
Antarctic Territories

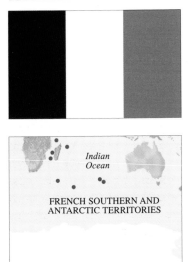

Flag proportions: 2:3
Adopted: n/a
Capital: Port-aux-Français
Area: 439,824 km2
(169,818 sq. mi)
Population: No permanent

settlement
Language: French
Religion: n/a
Currency: n/a
Exports: n/a

The French Southern and Antarctic Territories, which has no permanent population and is administered from Paris, flies the flag of France. The territory has five units: Adélie Land, Amsterdam and Saint Paul, Crozet Archipelago, Iles Eparses and Kerguelen. The French claim to Terre Adélie, which is part of Antarctica, is not internationally recognized. French sovereignty over the other territories is recognized, although Madagascar claims the Iles Eparses. Kerguelen is a bleak archipelago in the southern Indian Ocean. The territory also includes the Crozet Archipelago and the islands of Amsterdam and Saint Paul. In 2007, the Iles Eparses, five tiny island territories near Madagascar, were also added to the Territories.

DE FACTO STATES

The world contains a small number of territories that are beyond the control of the countries of which they legally form a part. These territories have every appearance of being independent states, except that they have no international diplomatic recognition (although Turkey, alone, recognizes Northern Cyprus). These de facto states have governments that control their territory, flags, anthems, and all the other trappings of statehood – except the recognition for which they all strive.

NORTHERN CYPRUS

The Turkish Republic of Northern Cyprus

Flag proportions: 3:5
Adopted: 9 March 1984
Capital: Nicosia (Lefkosa)
Area: 3,355km² (1,295sq mi)
Population: 257,000

Languages: Turkish
Religion: Sunni Islam
Currency: Turkish lira
Exports: Citrus fruit, potatoes, grapes, wine.

Cyprus became a British crown colony in 1925. In the mid-1950s a guerrilla war, to seek union with Greece, led to its leaders being deported. Archbishop Makarios returned as president of an independent Greek-Turkish Cyprus, but the Turks favoured a federal state in northern Cyprus. General Grivas returned in 1971 and campaigned against Makarios' government. After Makarios was ousted in 1974, Turkish troops took control of the north, establishing a dividing line (now a UN buffer zone) and claiming about one-third of the island as a Turkish Cypriot area (recognized only by Turkey).

The flag of Northern Cyprus retains the white field of its southern counterpart, with the red crescent and star depicted between two horizontal red stripes.

PALESTINE (WEST BANK AND GAZA)

The Palestinian Territories

Flag proportions: 1:2
Adopted: 1 December 1964
Capital: Ramallah
Area: 6,257km² (2,416sq mi)
Population: 3,762,000

Languages: Arabic
Religion: Sunni Islam
Currency: Israeli New Sheqel
Exports: Olives, fruit, vegetables, flowers, limestone.

Occupation and imposed rule have long been part of Palestine's legacy. After the Ottoman Empire collapsed in 1918, the Holy Land was mandated to Britain, beginning a conflict that is still not resolved.

The present flag was first used by the Arab National Movement in 1917, readopted at the 1948 Palestinian conference in Gaza, and endorsed by the PLO in 1964. Green is for the Fatimid dynasty of North Africa, red represents the Hashemites, descendants of the Prophet Mohammed, and the black and white colours are symbols of mourning and remembrance.

Israel and the Palestine Authority

Following the collapse of the Ottoman Empire after World War I, Palestine and Jordan were mandated to Britain in 1922 by the League of Nations. In 1947, a United Nations Special Committee on Palestine partitioned the land between Jordan and Israel.

The 1948 creation of Israel was bitterly opposed by the Palestinian Arabs, who had been calling for an independent homeland since the turn of the century. Several wars followed, including the Six-Day War of 1967, during which Israel occupied the West Bank of the Jordan River (Jordanian territory) and the Gaza Strip (Egyptian). These areas, widely considered by Arabs to be part of Palestine, are regarded by Israel as being of strategic importance. Israeli settlements have since been established in both, leading to the Palestinian description of them as 'occupied territories'.

The Palestine Liberation Organization (PLO) came into being in 1964, seeking to bring about an independent state of Palestine. In 1993, the PLO and Israel signed a Declaration of Principles on self-rule for the West Bank and Gaza. After a five-year transition, Israel was to transfer powers to the Palestinian Authority, established in 1994 and formerly headed by Yasser Arafat. Despite attacks and reprisals on both sides, negotiations continued until the outbreak in 2000 of a second *intifadah* (holy war), which ended hopes of a peaceful settlement.

In 2005 Israel withdrew from Gaza, leaving it with an undefined legal status. In 2007 the militant Hamas movement seized control of Gaza, confining Fatah (the other significant political force in the Territories) control to the West Bank. Gaza and the West Bank are now effectively separate entities.

DNIESTER REPUBLIC

The Transnistrian Moldovan Republic

Flag proportions: 1:2
Adopted: 25 July 2000
Capital: Tiraspol
Area: 3,479 km²
(1,343sq mi)
Population: 550,000
Language: Russian,

Moldovan (Romanian)
Religion: non-religious (majority),
Russian Orthodox
Currency: Rouble
Exports: metals, agricultural
produce.

Legally part of Moldova, Transnistria is a narrow sliver of land between the River Dniester and the Ukrainian border. Prior to World War II, the region was part of Ukraine within the Soviet Union, and was largely inhabited by Russians and Ukrainians, with a Moldovan minority. The territory was added to the Soviet Moldavian republic, which declared independence as Moldova in 1991. In the same year, Transnistria declared its own independence. Russia and Moldova have agreed that Transnistria should be autonomous within Moldova. The unrecognized republic flies the flag of the former Soviet Moldavian republic, with a red field, a green horizontal stripe and the hammer and sickle in the canton.

ABKHAZIA

Republic of Abkhazia

Flag proportions: 1:2
Adopted: 23 July 1992
Capital: Suchumi
Area: 8,660 km² (3,344sq mi)
Population: 230,000
Language: Abkhaz,

Russian, Georgian
Religion: Non-religious (majority),
Russian and Georgian Orthodox
Currency: Russian rouble
Exports: Citrus fruit, tea and wine.

Abkhazia is legally part of Georgia, of which it has been an autonomous republic since 1931. Subsequent Georgian settlement in Abkhazia reduced the Abkhaz population to a minority. Tension increased in 1992, when Abkhazia attempted secession. In 1993 Georgian troops sent to pacify Abkhazia were defeated, and Georgian residents evicted. In 1999, Abkhazia unilaterally declared independence. The republic remains a flashpoint and, although Russia does not recognize Abkhazia, the Russian authorities unofficially offer support. The flag of Abkhazia has a red canton carrying an open hand (an ancient Abkhaz symbol). The seven green and white stripes represent the seven traditional Abkhaz regions.

SOUTH OSSETIA

South Ossetia

Flag proportions: 1:2
Adopted: November 1990
Capital: Tskhinvali
Area: 3,900 km²
(1,505sq mi)
Population: 70,000

Language: Ossetian, Russian
Religion: Non-religious (majority),
Russian Orthodox
Currency: Russian rouble
Exports: Consumer goods.

Like Abkhazia, South Ossetia is legally part of Georgia, and was an autonomous republic until the Georgian authorities abolished its status in 1990. A revolt broke out in 1990 when Ossetians, wishing to unite with the North Ossetians in Russia, fought Georgian forces. Since 1992, under a Russo-Georgian agreement, Russian peacekeepers have been deployed between Georgia and South Ossetia. As a result, the region is beyond the control of Georgia and, effectively, independent. South Ossetia has a horizontal tricolour of white (representing spiritual life), red (military bravery) and yellow (the well-being of the Ossetian people).

KARABAKH (OR ARTSAKH)

Republic of Karabakh

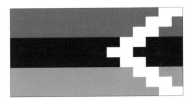

Flag proportions: 1:2
Adopted: 1995
Capital: Stepanakert
Area: 4,400 km²
(1,700sq mi)
Population: 138,000

Language: Armenian
Religion: Armenian Apostolic
(Orthodox)
Currency: Armenian Dram
Exports: Agricultural produce.

Peopled by Armenians, Karabakh, formerly Nagorno Karabakh, is legally an autonomous republic within Azerbaijan. The territory has been disputed by the Armenians and Azeris for more than a century. Ethnic violence spread in the territory in the late 1980s in the last years of the Soviet era, and Azeris fled from the region. As the Soviet Union broke up, Karabakh declared its independence as Artsakh. A war between Azerbaijan and ethnic Armenians began and, at the Russian-brokered cease-fire in 1994, Karabakh remained under Armenian control. The state's flag is that of Armenia, with a white arrow symbolically pointing towards Armenia, with which the region seeks unification.

WESTERN SAHARA

The Democratic Sahrawi Arab Republic

Flag proportions: 1:2
Adopted: 27 February 1976
Capital: Laayoune (Moroccan name; the city is de facto a Moroccan city), or El-Aaiun (the Sahrawi name; the name used by the exiled government)

Area: 266,000km² (102,700sq mi)
Population: 417,000
Language: Arabic
Religion: Sunni Islam
Currency: Moroccan dirham
Exports: Phosphates.

Morocco annexed all of Western Sahara as of 1979. (Mauritania had claimed some of the territory, but relinquished it under pressure from the Polisario Front liberation movement.) A guerilla war contesting Moroccan sovereignty ended in 1991 with a UN-brokered ceasefire, but the territory remains in dispute. The flag, in Pan-Arab colours, comprises a horizontal tricolour of equal bands of black, white and green with a red equilateral triangle at the hoist. In the white band are the Islamic crescent and star in red. Red represents the blood shed in the struggle for independence, black is for the period of colonization, white is for peace, while green stands for progress.

SOMALILAND

Republic of Somaliland

Flag proportions: 1:2
Adopted: 1996
Capital: Hargeysa
Area: 176,118 km² (68,000sq mi)
Population: 4,500,000

Language: Somali
Religion: Sunni Islam
Currency: Somaliland shilling
Exports: Sheep and goats, camels and cattle, hides, qat.

Internationally unrecognized, Somaliland has the same borders as the former colony of British Somaliland, which became independent in June 1960, four days before neighbouring Italian Somaliland, with which it merged to form Somalia. Since a coup in 1991, Somalia has had no effective government. However, a congress in the former British Somaliland repealed its union with Somalia and the region has since had a functioning government and infrastructure (unlike Somalia). Voters in Somaliland backed independence in a referendum in 2001. Somaliland's flag is a horizontal green, white and red tricolour with a black five-pointed star in the centre (the five points represent the five Somali regions). The *shahada*, the Islamic declaration of faith, is on the green stripe.

Glossary

Armorial banner Flag bearing an exact depiction of a coat of arms.

Arms Heraldic symbols of honour, granted to families, states, organizations etc.

Becket Short line attached to the hoist, with a toggle at the top and an eye splice or grommet at the bottom.

Blue peter Signal flag for the letter P, flown by a vessel about to leave port.

Canton The uppermost corner of the flag, nearest the hoist or flagpole.

Chief The upper portion (one third) of a heraldic shield.

Cleat Two-pronged fastener on the staff, within reach of the person securing the halyard by looping it over the cleat several times.

Cockade A coloured ribbon worn on caps to show political persuasion.

Compartment In heraldry, a panel or base below the shield, on which supporters sometimes stand.

Counter-change To place one design or pattern on top of another so that the underneath image remains visible.

Couped A cross cut cleanly, usually before reaching a border, like the cross on the flag of Switzerland.

Crest In heraldry, an object placed above a helmet on a shield.

Cross On a flag, a vertical and horizontal stripe placed at right angles, extending across the whole flag to divide it into four.

Dexter The right-hand side of a shield or coat of arms (the side opposite the left hand of the observer).

Ensign Rectangular flag flown at the stern of a vessel to denote its nationality. The ensign may differ from the national flag.

Field The whole of the flag or shield surface. When a design is applied, the field is effectively the background.

Flag Day June 14, an annual holiday in the USA, to celebrate the adoption in 1777 of the Stars and Stripes.

Flag of convenience Flag of a country in which a ship is registered for the sake of legal or financial advantage.

Flag officer Naval officer of the rank of Rear Admiral or above.

Flag of truce White flag raised on a battlefield indicating willingness to negotiate or surrender.

Flagship A naval warship on which the fleet commander is based. In a merchant fleet, usually the newest or most impressive ship.

Fly That part of the flag farthest from the staff, sometimes divided as upper fly and lower fly.

Garrison flag Large US flag flown on military posts on special days.

Gonfalon (gonfanon) A banner hanging from a crossbar; also a flag with three or more tails.

Guidon Cavalry A long, narrow flag with two rounded tails.

Half-mast A prescribed position below the full height of the flagstaff, but not necessarily halfway, at which a flag is flown as a sign of mourning.

Halyard The rope by which the flag is hoisted or lowered, with a toggle at one end and an eye splice or grommet at the other.

Heraldry Armorial bearings, insignia or symbols representing a person, family or dynasty. Also the study of the classification of these items and the allocation of the right to bear arms.

Hoist That part of the flag nearest to the staff, sometimes divided as upper hoist and lower hoist.

House flag Flag of a commercial undertaking.

Jack Rectangular national flag, smaller than the ensign, flown from the jackstaff.

Jackstaff Short staff at the bow of a warship, for flying the national flag. A jackstay is a wire rope to which the edge of a sail is fastened.

Labarum Standard or banner carried in Christian religious processions; also the military standard bearing a Christian monogram, once used by Constantine the Great.

Maritime flag Flag flown by civilian ships, usually from the stern or rear-mast. Also called a civil ensign, merchant ensign or merchant flag.

Mast Vertically fixed pole on a ship, for attaching the rigging. The term is also generally used, as in radio mast.

Metals In heraldry, gold (or) and silver (argent), often represented as yellow and white respectively.

Motto Word(s) or short sentence accompanying arms, often written in Latin or medieval French.

Naval ensign Flag flown by naval vessels and at naval bases. Often plain-coloured or of a simple right-angle cross design, with the national flag in the canton (*see also* Ensign, Maritime flag).

Obverse The 'front' of a flag, usually identical to the back or reverse.

Pennant Long, tapering or triangular flag flown from the masthead of a warship in commission.

Pile In heraldry, the shape of a wedge, usually point downward.

Post flag Large US flag normally flown on military posts.

Proper In heraldry, displayed in natural colours.

Proportion A flag's proportion is the ratio between the vertical depth (width) and the horizontal length.

Q-flag Quarantine flag. The yellow signal flag for the letter Q, flown from a vessel to indicate there is no disease on board and request permission to enter port. Also called a yellow flag.

Red Ensign Flag (ensign) of the British Merchant Navy.

Red Flag Flag with a red field and hammer and sickle emblem in the chief canton. First used during the French Revolution, it became the flag of Russia after the 1917 Bolshevik Revolution, then of the Soviet Union. It remains the flag of extreme left-wing political organizations.

Saltire A diagonal cross stretching from corner to corner of a flag.

State flag Flag flown by government and diplomatic missions abroad.

Tricolour A flag with three bands and three different colours, either horizontal or vertical.

Vexillology The study and collection of information about flags.

Index

A

Abkhazia (de facto state) 182

Afghanistan 69

Africa 149

Africa and Adjacent Islands 149–179

African National Congress (ANC) 21

Alabama 112

Aland (Aland Islands) 40 and Finland and Sweden 40

Alaska 112

Albania 51

Alderney 31

Algeria 151

American Samoa 102, 103 see also Samoa

Andorra 34

Angola 149, 171

Anguilla 125

Antarctica 146 French Southern and Antarctic Territories 179

Antigua and Barbuda 126

Argentina 139, 146

Arizona 112

Arkansas 112

Armenia 57 and Karabakh (Artsakh) 183

Artsakh see Karabakh

Aruba 135

Ascension Island 179

Asia: Eastern and Southeast 77–89 Western and Southern 61–75

Association of Southeast Asian Nations (ASEAN) 23

Australia 91, 94, 95 state flags of 95

Australian Capital Territory (ACT) 95

Austria 42, 45

Azerbaijan 58

B

Bahamas 120

Bahrain 11, 67 and Qatar 67

Bangladesh 73 eastern province of Pakistan 74

banners 14, 15–17, 19, 21, 44

Barbados 130

Belarus 11, 56 and Soviet Byelorussia 56

Belgian Congo 165

Belgium 35 Belgian administration and Rwanda 165

Belize (British Honduras) 119

Benin (kingdom of Dahomey) 159

Bermuda 116

Bhutan 74

Bird Island 147

Blue Ensign 94, 95, 100, 101, 104–6, 116, 121, 122, 125, 127, 146–7, 177, 179

Bohemia 43

Bolivia 139, 144

Bonaire 133

Bosnia and Herzegovina 48

Bosnia and Herzegovina Federation 48

Republic of Srpska 48

Botswana 149, 173

Brazil 143

Britain 23, 126 and British Commonwealth of Nations 23 and colonies 126, 127

British Antarctic Territory 18

British Honduras see Belize

British Indian Ocean Territory 177

British Virgin Islands (BVI) 125 and St Kitts and Nevis 126

Brunei 87

Bulgaria 53

Burkina Faso 160

Burma see Myanmar

Burundi 166

C

California 112

Cambodia 84

Cameroon 162

Canada 109, 114

Cape Verde 155 islands 156

Caribbean 109, 111, 118, 119, 120, 121, 122, 123, 124, 125, 126, 127, 128, 129, 130, 131, 132, 133, 134, 135

Cayman Bric 122

Cayman Islands 122 Jamaican dependency 122

Central African Republic (Ubangi-Shari) 162

Central America 109,111 United Provinces of 117, 118, 119

Chad 161 and Romanian flag 161

Channel Islands 32

Chile 145

China 77, 79, 80 and Hong Kong 79 and Macau 80

Christmas Island 89

coats of arms 14, 15, 16,
    17, 19, 87, 101
Cocos (Keeling) Islands
    89
Colombia 139, 140, 141
Colorado 112
Commonwealth 23, 86,
    99, 101, 141, 154,
    161, 169, 178
Comoros 176
Congo-Brazzaville 164
Connecticut 112
Cook Islands 106
Costa Rica 119
Côte d'Ivoire 157
    and Niger flag 160
Council of Europe 23
Croatia 48
Cuba 121
Curaçao 132, 133
Cyprus 52
Czech Republic 43
Czechoslovakia *see*
    Czech Republic;
    Slovakia

D

Dahomey, kingdom of
    see Benin
de facto states 180–184
    Abkhazia 182
    Dniester Republic 182
    Karabakh (or Artsakh)
    183
    Northern Cyprus 180

Palestine 181
Somaliland 184
South Ossetia 183
Western Sahara 184
Delaware 112
Democratic Republic of
    the Congo (Zaire) 165
Denmark 37, 38,
    115, 124
Diego Garcia (island) 177
District of Columbia 112
Djibouti (French Somaliland;
    Territory of the Afars
    and Issas) 167
Dniester Republic
    (de facto state) 182
Dominica 129
Dominican Republic 124
Dutch East India Company
    20

E

East Timor 88
Ecuador 139, 140
Egypt 11, 149, 153, 166
    and Iraq 68
El Salvador 13, 118
England 19, 30
Equatorial Guinea
    (Spanish Guinea) 163
Eritrea 167
    and Ethiopia 167
Estonia 41
Ethiopia 158, 168
Europe 27–58

European Union (EU) 22,
    23, 29, 155
    and Council of
    Europe 23

F

Faeroes, The 37; *see*
    also Denmark
Falkland Islands 137, 146
    and Argentina 146
    Falkland Island
    Dependencies 18
Federation of Arab
    Republics (Egypt, Libya
    and Syria) 152, 153
Fiji 101
Finland 11, 40
    and Aland 40
flags:
    burning 21
    display 10–11
    disposal of 11
    draping 11
    flying 10–13
    at funerals 11, 12–13
    at half-mast 11, 12, 13
    hanging vertically 11
    history 14–21
    hoisting 12
    hours for flying 11
    military colours 10
    in mourning 12–13
    multinational displays
    12
    national 10,11,

12–13, 56
    saluting 13
    senior position 22
    size 12
    two sides of 13
    upside down 12
    uses 11
Florida 112
France 19, 20, 34, 35
    and Algeria 151
    and Cambodia 84
    and Comoros 176
    and Chad 161
    and Italy 45
    and Lebanon 63
    and Morocco 151
    Overseas Territories
    34, 101
French Congo 164
French Cotentin peninsula
    31
French Equitorial Africa
    161, 164
French Guiana 142
French Polynesia 34, 104
French Somaliland
    see Djibouti
French Southern and
    Antarctic Territories 179
French West Africa 157

G

Gabon 164
Gambia, (The) 154
Georgia, Republic of 57

and Abkhazia 182
and South Ossetia 183
Georgia (USA) 113
Germany (Federal
   Republic of Germany)
   20–21, 43
and East Germany 43
and West Germany 43
Ghana (Gold Coast) 158
Gibraltar 33
Gilbert and Ellice Islands
   103
Grand Cayman 122
Greece 51
Greenland 115
   see also Denmark
Grenada 131
Guadeloupe 127
Guam 96
Guatemala 111, 117
Guernsey 31
Guinea (French Guinea) 155
Guinea-Bissau 156
Guyana 141

H
Haiti 123
Hawaii 113
Henderson Islands *see*
   Pitcairn Islands
Honduras 117
Hong Kong 79
Hungary 54

I
Iceland 38
Idaho 113

Illinois 113
India 61, 72, 73
Indiana 113
Indochina 83, 84
Indonesia 11, 88, 89
International Committee of
   the Red Cross *see*
   Red Cross
international organizations
   22–23
Iowa 113
Iran 69
Iraq 68
Ireland 30
Isle of Man 32
Israel 64
   and the Palestine
   Authority 181
Italy 45

J
Jamaica 122
   and Ethiopian colours
   168
Japan 81, 84, 99
Java 89
Jersey 31
Jordan 64

K
Kansas 113
Karabakh (or Artsakh;
   formerly Nagorno
   Karabakh; de facto
   state) 183
Kazakhstan 71
Kentucky 113

Kenya 169
Kiribati 103
Klein Curaçao 132
Kosovo 49
Kuwait 68
Kyrgyzstan 72

L
Laos 84
Latin America *see* South
   America
Latvia 41
League of Nations 181;
   see also United Nations
Lebanon 63
Leeward Islands 104, 126
Lesotho (Basutoland) 175
Liberia 157
Libya 152
   and Federation of Arab
   Republics 152
Liechtenstein 44
   and Haitian flag 44
Lithuania 42
Little Cayman 122
Louisiana 113
Luxembourg 35, 36

M
Macau 80
Macedonia 50
Madagascar 175, 179
Maine 113
Malawi 170, 171
Malaysia 86
Maldives 75
Mali 159

and Senegalese
   flag 154
Malta 47
Mariana Islands 96
Marshall Islands 97
Martinique 129
Maryland 113
Mascarene Islands 178
Massachusetts 113
Mauritania 153
Mauritius 178
Mayotte 176
Mediterranean 33, 52
Mexico 109, 111, 116
Michigan 113
Micronesia 97
   Federated States of
   Micronesia 96, 97
Minnesota 113
Mississippi 113
Missouri 113
Moldova 55
   and Dniester Republic
   182
   and Transnistria 182
Monaco 11, 35
Mongolia 81
Montana 113
Montenegro 50
Montserrat 127
Morocco 13, 151
Mozambique 172
Myanmar (Burma) 85

N
Nagorno Karabakh *see*
   Karabakh

Namibia 149, 173
NATO 27
Nauru 98
Nebraska 113
Nepal 74
Netherlands, The
19, 20, 35, 36, 128,
132, 134
and Aruba 135
and Dutch colony 88
and Netherlands
Antilles 133,
134, 135
Nevada 113
New Caledonia 100
New Hampshire 113
New Hebrides *see*
Vanuatu
New Jersey 113
New Mexico 113
New South Wales 95
New York State 113
New Zealand 91, 92–93,
101, 104, 105, 106
Nicaragua 118
Niger 160
Nigeria 161
Niue 106
Normandy 31
North America 109, 110
North Carolina 113
North Dakota 113
North Korea 82, 83
Northern Cyprus (de facto
state) 180
Northern Mariana islands
94

Northern Rhodesia *see*
Zambia
Northern Territory 95
Norway 11, 38
Svalbard 39

O
Oceania 91
Ohio 113
Oklahoma 113
Oman 66
Orange Free State 21
Oregon 113
Ottoman Empire 48, 49,
50, 51, 52, 53, 57,
58, 65, 149, 181
Ottomans 67

P
Pakistan 72; *see also*
Bangladesh
Palau 96
Palestine (West Bank and
Gaza; de facto state)
181
Israel and the Palestine
Authority, box on 181
PLO (Palestine
Liberation Organization)
181
Panama 120
Papua New Guinea
(PNG) 98
Paraguay 139, 144
Pennsylvania 113
Peru 143
Philippines 77, 87

Pitcairn Islands 104
Poland 11, 42
Portugal 32
and Angola 171
and Brazil 143
and Macau 80
and Sao Tomé and
Príncipe 163
Puerto Rico 123
and USA 123

Q
Qatar 67
and Bahrain 67
Queensland 95

R
Red Cross (International
Committee of the Red
Cross) 23
Red Crystal 23
Republic of the Congo
see Congo-Brazzaville
Réunion 34, 178
Rhode Island 113
Romania 11, 53
and Chad flag 161
Russia 42, 56
Rwanda 165

S
Saba 134
Saint-Barthélemy 128
Saint Eustatius (also
known as Sint Eustatius
and Statia) 134
Saint Helena 179

St Kitts and Nevis (also
St Christopher and
Nevis) 126
Saint Lucia 129, 130
Saint Martin 128
Saint-Martin 128
Sint Maarten 128
St Pierre et Miquelon 115
Saint Vincent and the
Grenadines 131
saltire 18, 30, 31, 115
Samoa (Western Samoa)
102
and American Samoa
102, 103
San Marino 46
Sao Tomé and Príncipe
163
Sark 31
Saskatchewan 16, 18
Saudi Arabia 65
and Bahrain 67
Senegal 154
and Mali flag 154
Serbia 49
Serbia and Montenegro
49, 50
Seychelles 177
Sierra Leone 156
Singapore 86
Sint Maarten 131
Slovakia 54
and Czechoslovakia
54; *see also* Czech
Republic
Slovenia 47
Solomon Islands 99

Somalia 168, 184
Somaliland (de facto
   state) 184
South Africa 21, 149,
   174
South America 137–147
South Australia 95
South Carolina 114
South Dakota 114
South Georgia and South
   Sandwich Islands 16, 147
South Korea 82, 83
South Ossetia (de facto
   state) 183
Southern Cross 89,
   94–95, 98, 102,
   105, 146
Southern Rhodesia *see*
   Zimbabwe
Spain 13, 33, 34,
   117, 135
Spanish Guinea *see*
   Equitorial Guinea
'Spice Island' *see*
   Grenada
Spitsbergen 39
Sri Lanka 75
Sudan 166
Suriname 142
Svalbard 39
   and Norway 39
   and Spitsbergen 39
Swaziland 174
Sweden 39
   and Aland 40
Switzerland 44
Syria 63, 68

T
Taiwan 80
Tajikistan 71
Tanganyika 170
Tanzania 170
Tasmania 95
Tennessee 114
Territory of the Afars
   and Issas *see* Djibouti
Texas 114
Thailand 85
Togo 158
Togoland 158
Tokelau 105
Tonga 102
Transvaal 21
Tricolore 20, 30,
   34, 38, 101
   see also France
Trinidad and Tobago 132
Tristan da Cunha group
   179
Tunisia 152
Turkey 52
   Northern Cyprus 180
   Turkish Republic of
   Northern Cyprus 52
Turkmenistan 70
Turks and Caicos 121
Tuvalu 100

U
Ubangi-Shari *see* Central
   African Republic
Uganda 169
Ukraine 55

Union Flag (Union Jack)
   11, 30, 106, 116
   see also Blue Ensign
United Arab Emirates
   (UAE) 66
United Kingdom (UK) 30
United Nations (UN)
   23, 27, 49, 88
   UN trust territory 98
Uruguay 139, 145
USA (United States of
   America) 11, 20, 109,
   111, 112, 124, 145
   and Puerto Rico 123
   states 112–14
US Trust Territory of the
   Pacific Islands 96, 97
Utah 114
Uzbekistan 70

V
Vanuatu (New Hebrides)
   99
Vatican City 46
Venezuela 139, 141
Vermont 114
Victoria 95
Vietnam 83
Virgin Islands 124
   see also British Virgin
   Islands
Virginia 114

W
Wales 17
Wallachia 53

Wallis and Futuna 101
Washington (state) 114
West Bank and Gaza *see*
   Palestine
West Pakistan 73
West Virginia 114
Western Australia 16,
   18, 95
Western Sahara (de facto
   state) 184
   and Mauritania 184
   and Morocco 184
Western Samoa *see*
   Samoa
Windward Islands 104
Wisconsin 114
Wyoming 114

Y
Yemen 65
Yugoslavia 11, 47, 48,
   49, 50

Z
Zaire *see* Democratic
   Republic of the
   Congo
Zambia (Northern
   Rhodesia) 171
Zanzibar 170
Zimbabwe (Southern
   Rhodesia) 172